Woodworking
for
Beginners

*Learn the Fundamentals of
Woodworking, From the Tools
at Your Disposal to the
Techniques You'll Use Most
Often
(2022 Guide for Newbies)*

Maxwell Field

TABLE OF CONTENT

INTRODUCTION

My first experience with finishing furniture was typical of most woodworkers: I applied varnish with a brush, and the results were less than spectacular. Finally, I discovered wipe-on finishes, which produced a more appealing result.

Nonetheless, I found the procedure to be slow, and the available finishes to be limited. So, I decided to learn how to spray finish early on. I was familiar with the procedure and knew how good the results could be because I had some experience painting carriages.

After many compressors and spray guns, I can now say that I am competent at spraying finishes. While the path to mastery was paved with drips and runs, spray finishing was no more difficult than many of the other woodworking techniques I've learned.

I can honestly say that, unlike many woodworkers who still struggle with rags and brushes, I enjoy finishing. The tools are enjoyable to use, and I am pleased with the results.

Various woodworkers are wary of spraying finishes because they are concerned about the additional tools required, ventilation, overspray, dust issues, learning curve, and so on.

However, if you stick to water-based finishes, you can get by with just a few basic tools: a midsize compressor, a gravity-feed HVLP gun, and an inexpensive window fan. Because of their flammability, solvent-based finishes must be sprayed with explosion-proof light fixtures and exhaust fan motors. The only exception is if you work outside and are not near any source of ignition.

In this book, we will look at project finishing preparation, oil, and varnish blends, water-based finishes, how to prepare the surface, and how to choose an application technique. Following that, we will look at the application of Water-based finishes, sanding techniques, hand-sanding techniques, tabletop flattening, and curve shaping are all examples of techniques.

Following that, we'll look at spray finishing, spraying advantages, and spraying costs. How to use a spray gun, high-pressure spray tools such as HVLP spray systems and vacuum motor spray rigs, touch-up spray guns, spraying setup, spraying basics, and spraying furniture. Following that, we'll look at thinning finishes and using the proper solvent gloves, aerosol finishes, accurate technique yields, sanding and priming, clear coating & rubbing out, steps to painted finishing, filling and sanding, glazing techniques, glaze coats, and how to use wood bleach.

Following that, we'll go over polished finishing techniques, decorative finishing techniques, stenciling techniques, graining techniques, French polishing techniques, marbling techniques, rubbing techniques, and protective finishing techniques. Next, we'll go over what other tools and accessories you'll need, as well as how to choose a protective finish, how to use polyurethane, how to use shellac, and how to use lacquer.

Finally, we'll go over how to finish by hand, as well as some tips on proper cleaning and storage procedures. Let's get started if you're ready!

Chapter One

Project Finishing Preparation

Finishing is one of the most difficult problems for most woodworkers. Despite the discomfort caused by complex joinery or intricate and precise machining, many woodworkers shudder at the thought of applying a finish to their work.

What is the best way to end a project? This is a question I am frequently asked. It is critical to be able to confidently answer that question.

Waxes, oils, varnishes, shellacs, lacquers, and water-based finishes can be divided into manageable categories based on general working qualities and the degrees of protection they provide.

Different finishes provide varying degrees of protection, resilience, ease of application, reparability, and appeal.

Unfortunately, no single finish excels in all categories. A finish that excels in one category may fail in another, which you must accept as a trade-off.

As a professional refinisher, I routinely ask my a series of questions to my customers to determine the best finish for their furniture.

I've modified my standard questions and added a few as a checklist for woodworkers deciding which finish to use on their projects.

The answers to these questions will point you in the direction of the best finish to use on a particular project, based on how well you need to protect the surface, how well the finish will hold up, how easy it is to apply, and how you want it to look.

Let's start with the different types of wood finishes to get a better understanding of the options. Based on how they dry or cure, all wood finishes can be classified into one of two distinct types.

Lacquer, shellac, and other water-based finishes evaporatively dry to a hard film as the solvents evaporate. As a side note Water is not a solvent; rather, it serves as a carrier for the finished emulsion.

These finishes will always redissolve in the solvent used to thin them, even after they have dried, making them less durable than reactive finishes.

Most reactive finishes, such as linseed or tung oil, catalyzed lacquers, and varnishes, contain solvents that evaporate, but they cure by reacting to either air outside the can or a chemical placed inside the can before application.

These finishes undergo a chemical change as they cure, and they will not dissolve in the solvent used to thin them again. Except for pure oils, reactive finishes are more resistant to heat and compounds.

I don't think wax is an appropriate finish, and I only use paste wax to polish furniture over other finishes like lacquer or shellac. Linseed oil and tung oil are drying oils that are commonly used in finishing and are readily available and relatively inexpensive.

These finishes are referred to as true oils to distinguish them from other products marketed as oil finishes and to distinguish them from naturally nondrying or semi-drying oils used in finishes, such as soybean oil.

Polymerization, a process that strengthens the cured finish, converts these true oils from a liquid to a solid. Linseed oil is available in a variety of forms.

Unrefined linseed oil, also known as raw linseed oil, is rarely used on wood because it dries so slowly. Finishers long ago discovered that boiling the oil produced a denser, faster-drying product.

Even though boiled linseed oil is still available, it is referred to as heat-treated or polymerized oil. The majority of the Boiled linseed oil sold nowadays is raw oil that has been chemically treated.

These will hasten the drying process. Only boiled linseed oil should be used for wood finishing. Tung oil is extracted from the nuts of trees native to Asia but cultivated in other parts of the world.

Tung oil is available in two forms: pure, unrefined oil and heat-treated or polymerized oil. The heat-treating procedure strengthens the oil and shortens the drying time. It also reduces tung oil's tendency to "frost" (dry to a whitish, matte appearance). Tung oil is lighter in color and more resistant to moisture than linseed oil.

Both licensed and tung oils are penetrating finishes, meaning they penetrate the wood fibers and harden. These are the simplest finishes to use.

Wipe them on, allow them to penetrate the wood's surface, and then wipe away the excess with a rag. Because the film is too soft, these oils are usually not built up with enough coats to form a surface film like varnish or lacquer.

Varnish is made of tough and long-lasting synthetic resins that have been treated with drying oils.

Labels on varnish cans will list resins like alkyd, phenolic, and urethane, as well as oils like tung and linseed, as well as other semi-drying oils like soybean and safflower.

Varnish cures use the same polymerization process as true oils, but the resins make this finish more durable than oil. Oil-based varnish is the most durable finish that the average woodworker can easily apply.

Varnish outperforms most other finishes in terms of resistance to water, heat, solvents, and other chemicals. Long-oil varnishes are varnishes that contain a high percentage of oil.

These include marine, spar, or exterior varnishes, as well as some retail interior varnishes. Long-oil varnishes are more elastic and softer than medium and short-oil varnishes, which contain less oil.

Most interior varnishes on the market are medium-oil varnishes. Short-oil varnishes, also known as heat-set varnishes and baking enamels, require extremely high drying temperatures and are therefore only used in industrial applications.

The characteristics of the finish are determined by the type of resin used in the varnish. Alkyd varnish is a common all-purpose interior diversity with adequate protective properties.

Phenolic varnish, which is typically made with tung oil, is primarily intended for exterior use. Urethane varnish, also known as polyurethane varnish, is more resistant to heat, solvents, and abrasions than any other varnish.

Varnish is typically applied with a brush, but wiping varnish, a highly thinned and gelled version, can be applied with a rag.

CHAPTER TWO

OIL AND VARNISH MIXTURES

These mixtures, which are mostly oil with a little varnish added, combine the best qualities of both ingredients: the ease of application of true oils and the protective qualities of varnish.

It's difficult to describe accurate protective qualities for these items because manufacturers rarely disclose the oil-to-varnish ratio. Oil-varnish blends dry a little harder than true oils, and the finishes build up faster with fewer applications.

While most people associate shellac with a liquid finish found in a paint store, it is a natural resin secreted by a bug that feeds on trees, primarily in India and Thailand.

The secretions are collected in the form of cocoons and eventually refined into dry flakes, which are then dissolved in denatured alcohol to make the shellac solution sold in cans at the store.

Shellac comes in a variety of colors. You can buy it pre-blended or in flake form and mix it with denatured alcohol yourself. The pre-blended variety is available in orange and clear, which is bleached shellac.

Shellac flakes are available in a wider range of colors and wax contents than the pre-blended version, which contains wax. The wax in shellac reduces water resistance and prevents some oil finishes from bonding to it.

Most professionals still consider lacquer to be the best all-around finish for wood because it dries quickly, adds incredible depth and richness to the wood, has moderate to excellent resilience, and rubs out well.

Lacquer comes in a variety of varieties, each with its own set of performance characteristics. The most common is nitrocellulose lacquer.

If the label says lacquer, it's most likely nitrocellulose, which is made by dissolving an alkyd and nitrocellulose resin and then blending it with solvents that evaporate quickly.

This lacquer is water resistant, but it is sensitive to heat and certain solvents. The main disadvantage is that the finish tends to be yellow as it ages, which is especially noticeable in light-colored woods.

Acrylic-modified lacquer is created by combining a non-yellowing cellulose resin known as cellulose acetate butyrate with acrylic.

This lacquer has the same general properties as nitrocellulose lacquer, except it is completely water-white, which means it will not appear amber when applied to light-colored woods.

Furthermore, the finish will not be yellow over time. Catalyzed lacquer bridges the gap between nitrocellulose lacquer's application characteristics and varnish's resilience.

Catalyzed lacquer is a complex finish made up of urea formaldehyde or urea melamine and an alkyd with nitrocellulose resin added to make it handle like regular lacquer.

The addition of an acid catalyst starts a chemical reaction that results in a very tough, long-lasting finish. There are two types of catalyzed lacquer: pre-catalyzed and post-catalyzed.

Pre-catalyzed lacquer has the components pre-blended, either by the manufacturer or when you buy it; post-catalyzed lacquer is a two-part system that you must mix in your shop, adhering to the precise ratios.

Once the catalyst is added, these lacquers have a relatively short shelf life or the amount of time they can be used.

CHAPTER THREE

WATER-BASED FINISHES

Water-based finishes contain some of the same ingredients as varnish and lacquer, most notably thane alkyd and acrylic, but water has replaced many flammable and polluting ingredients.

This product's chemistry is complicated. Because the resins have no natural affinity for water, they must be chemically modified or forced to combine with it.

Water-based finishes are typically created using either an acrylic resin (sold as water-based lacquer) or an acrylic urethane mixture (sold as water-based polyurethane).

The addition of urethane, like varnish, makes the resin tougher and more scratch-resistant, but water-based urethane lacks the solvent and heat resistance of its oil-based counterpart.

A finish's resilience is determined by its resistance to water, compounds, solvents (such as those found in alkaline cleaners and acidic foods), heat, and scratches.

If exposed to water for an extended period, wax, shellac, lacquer, and some water-based finishes will be damaged. Most of these items also scratch easily; however, they rub out well. That is the inverse of scratch resistance.

Wax is surprisingly acid and alkali resistant. Aside from that, it is the least long-lasting finish. Shellac is not resistant to alkalis such as ammonia or alcohol.

Lacquer, nitrocellulose and acrylic, water, and solvent-based evaporative finishes perform the best in terms of overall resilience.

The most durable hand-applied finish is oil-based polyurethane, and the most durable sprayed finishes are catalyzed lacquer and varnish.

CHAPTER FOUR

MATCH YOUR SKILL LEVEL

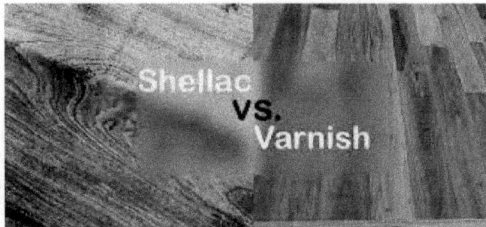

Your level of involvement, the environment in which you work, and whether you're set up to spray all have an impact on which finish you use.

Your choice will be influenced by the temperature and dampness of your surroundings, as well as the amount of sanding dust in the air. Dust falling onto a finish is less of an issue with lacquer or shellac than it is with a slow-drying finish like varnish.

Shellac and lacquer are also the least temperamental in cold temperatures, and they can be modified with retarder additives for hot and humid environments.

Oils and oil-based products dry slowly in cold and humid temperatures, and dust is always an issue when it has time to become embedded in the dried film.

To exhaust the overspray, spray tools require a larger budget and, in most cases, expensive tools. Spraying has a learning curve, so it will probably take some practice before you get good results.

Do you prefer a natural in-wood finish? Or does your project necessitate an elegant, deep, glass-smooth finish? Is the color of the finish an issue, or will they allow the finish cause problems in the future?

For a natural-looking finish, woodworkers have traditionally used oil, wax, or oil and varnish blends. None of these quick-drying finishes form a hard surface film.

However, you can achieve a natural-looking effect with any finish, including varnish, shellac, and lacquer, as long as you only apply a few coats and rub out the dried film with steel wool.

If you want a filled pore, deep, lustrous finish, use a hard, film-forming finish like varnish, shellac, or lacquer. This performs complex coloring options such as toning and glazing, and the type of finish is also required. The color of the finish and its penetration may be an issue.

Colors in orange shellac and phenolic-resin varnish may be too dark for woods that you want to keep as light as possible. Furthermore, various finishes deepen or darken the wood surface. In most cases, this is desirable because it adds depth and luster. Nonetheless, any deepening effect should be minimized.

When an oil finish is applied to some delicately figured woods, such as pear wood, the color will appear muddy. Oil and oil-based varnish, solvent-based lacquer, and shellac are the most effective at deepening the color of the wood and increasing surface luster

These finishes penetrate the surface and wet the wood. Other film finishes, particularly water-based finishes and some catalyzed lacquers, tend to float on the surface.

They make the wood appear lighter in color by not penetrating it as deeply. The plastic appearance that polyurethane and catalyzed lacquers occasionally exhibit is due to the incorrect application of these finishes rather than the finishes themselves.

The application of thick varnish and lacquer to open-pored woods, such as plain sawn ash or oak, can result in a soupy appearance on the surface. This is due to the finished film bridging across the open pores instead of flowing into them.

You can achieve more appealing results by thinning these finishes. My preferred method for applying oil-based polyurethane is to thin it 50% with mineral spirits and wipe it on. With unstained, light-colored woods like maple or birch, a finished film that yellows with age will be noticeable.

This is not a problem with a water- or solvent-based acrylic finish. Paste wax and some catalyzed finishes will not be yellow as well.

Application:

1.   Atomizing the finish into a fine spray allows you to achieve a smoother, more even finish faster than any other technique.Shellac and

oil-based varnishes, including polyurethane, as well as water-based, nitrocellulose, and catalyzed lacquers, can be sprayed.

1.   Using a brush to apply a coat of finish will require fewer applications, whether you use a disposable sponge brush or the more traditional bristles. Cautious technique means doing everything possible to achieve a neat job. Brushes are most effective with oil and water-based varnishes.

2.   Time-honored French polish is required, with several coats of shellac applied with a rag. This technique, which is time-consuming but nearly foolproof, can be used to apply oils as well as varnishes. Patience is required when wiping on a finish.

A solvent-based finish, such as varnish or lacquer, contains a significant number of organic solvents, which can harm the environment as well as your health. It's also extremely flammable.

If these details bother you, use a water-based finish to eliminate the fire hazard while also reducing the environmental and health impact.

Pure oil is a surprisingly effective substitute for solvent-based lacquer or vanishes:

Pure oil contains no solvents and is derived from renewable sources. However, oil-soaked rags must be disposed of with caution. Shellac is another viable option.

Denatured alcohol, the solvent for shellac, is distilled from corn, and most people don't mind the fleeting odor. Despite what you may have read or heard; all finishes are nontoxic when fully cured.

Any cured film is safe to contact with food once the solvents have evaporated. This does not imply that the finish is safe to consume. It simply means that additives like heavy-metal driers and plasticizers are sufficiently encapsulated so that they do not migrate into your food.

Except for mineral oil, which is sold as a laxative, the only edible finishes I'm aware of are wax and shellac. Spraying wastes a lot of the finished material and disperses the organic solvents into the air. Brushing or wiping on a finish is a practical, albeit slower, option.

Using Waterborne Paints

Before I had spray tools, I applied solvent-based finishes with brushes or rags.

I had a limited budget and very little shop space when I finally bought a spray gun, so I couldn't set up an appropriate spray booth.

I looked for non-flammable and relatively safe finishes. The obvious choice was waterborne lacquers. All I needed was a fan to circulate the air and a clean area to spray.

It took some trial and error, but I'm now getting consistent even coats of finish that are smooth and defect-free. I've also discovered that I don't need to use spray tools to achieve satisfactory results.

A variety of waterborne finishes can be applied successfully with brushes or pads. Even though I now have the tools to spray solvent-based lacquers and varnishes, I still use waterborne finishes 90% of the time.

Many states now limit the number of solvents or volatile organic compounds that professional shops can emit into the air. As a result, more user-friendly and less toxic waterborne finishes have been developed.

However, waterborne products differ significantly from solvent-based counterparts. They can be frustrating to work with and produce disappointing results if they are not used correctly. Knowing what issues to expect and how to overcome them will make applying waterborne finishes easier.

Surface preparation, compatibility of sealers, stains, and topcoats; material preparation; application techniques; and even the weather all play a role in success. My methods work with waterborne urethanes, lacquers, dyes, sealers, and primers.

Chapter Five

Surface Preparation

If you've ever spilled water on freshly sanded wood, you've probably noticed how the grain stands up and creates a rough surface. On wood, all waterborne finishes have this effect.

Grain-raising isn't as bad as it used to be because older types contained more water than newer formulations. Today's resins are lighter and more viscous, requiring less water in their formulations.

However, no matter how much bare wood you sand, all waterborne finishes will raise the grain enough to require some additional sanding. Surrendering to raised grain is the simplest way to deal with it.

Finish-sand work pieces as usual with sandpaper in the ISO-grit to the 220-grit range, then intentionally raise the grain. Water, sanding sealer, or dewaxed shellac can all be used.

If you use water, dampen a sponge or rag lightly and wipe the workpiece. You can also use a plant mister to dampen the wood. Allow the workpiece to dry completely before sanding with 220- to 400-grit paper.

When applied to this surface, a waterborne finish will not significantly raise the grain. Light sanding is required after the first coat, but this is also required when using a solvent-based finish. Instead of water, I usually raise the grain with a coat of sanding sealer.

Most manufacturers provide sealers designed specifically for their products. Sealers are typically formulated with stearates, which act as lubricants and facilitate sanding.

If you can't find a sealer, shellac will do the trick. If the wood needs to be colored, I apply one coat of water-soluble dye to bring out the grain, followed by a coat of sealer or shellac.

Sand it after it has dried. The sealer or shellac stiffens the dyed fibers, making them much easier to sand. The sealer also acts as a buffer, preventing you from quickly sanding through the dye to bare wood.

The amount of grain raised varies depending on the type of wood. Open-grain woods like oak will require more sanding than closed-grain wood like maple.

Depending on how fine a surface I want, I use wet or dry sandpaper in the 220- to the 400-grit range. I don't use stearate-containing sandpapers.

When waterborne finishes are applied over small stearate particles that have not been cleaned off the workpiece surface, they cause surface defects known as fisheyes. After sanding, wipe away the dust with a damp, lint-free cloth.

The workpiece will be dry enough for a finish by the time you get out your brushes or set up your spray tools. Tack rags should not be used because the resins in them can react with the finish and leave blemishes.

Waterborne top coats must be compatible with any fillers, stains, or dyes used. The majority of waterborne materials have improved, and many are now compatible with solvent-based goods.

That is not to say that all materials will be compatible in all situations.
Allow enough time for the oil-based product to cure before applying waterborne lacquer over it, for example.

Rough up the surface with very fine grit sandpaper before applying the waterborne product, so the first coat has a better chance of biting into the stain.

On occasion, two pieces of merchandise immediately demonstrate their incompatibility, and the top coat will bead up or not flow out. Blistering, for example, can manifest several days later.

Experiment on a scrap of material if you're unsure about compatibility. Applying a barrier coat of sealer between two items is the simplest way to eliminate any doubt about their compatibility.

Dewaxed shellac is the best sealer I've found. While you can buy shellac that has had the wax removed, also known as blond shellac, it is difficult to find and usually comes in large quantities.

I buy clear, pre-blended shellac in 3-pound increments and leave it alone for a day or two until the wax settles to the bottom of the can. The clear top fluid is then poured off. I dilute it with denatured alcohol to a ratio of 2:1.

Then I sand lightly with 220-grit or finer paper after applying a fairly heavy, even coat of this. The shellac not only seals in the first coat but also aids in the bonding of two potentially incompatible materials. It's never let me down.

Finishing Materials should be thoroughly mixed and strained. Most waterborne finishes are designed to be applied directly from the can and do not require thinning. The only thing you have to do before using them is stir up the solids that have settintod to the bottom of the can.

These solids tend to separate or settle out over time and may require vigorous stirring to return to the solution. The older the material, the more likely lumps are present.

Finally, I strain it through plastic, paper, or nylon mesh filter as a precaution. When a finish, such as a thick, pigmented primer, does not flow or spray well, you may need to thin it.

Waterborne finishes are extremely sensitive and do not respond to thinning, in contrast to traditional nitrocellulose lacquers, which can be thinned almost indefinitely.

Waterborne materials are made up of carefully measured amounts of various compounds such as solvents, water, defoaming agents, and resins. Introducing another material into the mix can throw the balance off.

Because it takes too long to dry, the finish may be prone to runs and drips. If the finish does not flow properly after brushing, contact the manufacturer to see if a flow additive is available.

As a last resort, try adding small amounts in the range of 3% to 5% by volume of clean water. Although distilled water is preferred, I have used plain tap water with no adverse effects.

If the finish appears to be too dry when spraying in hot, dry conditions, you should add a retarder or the surface will look and feel fuzzy.

CHAPTER SIX

CHOOSING AN APPLICATION TECHNIQUE

Waterborne topcoats designed for spraying differ from those designed for brushing or padding. A spray finish is exactly what it sounds like. Brushing it may cause the material to foam or dry too quickly.

However, I've discovered that any brush able finish can be sprayed with good results. Most waterborne stains and dyes do not require any special preparation application tools and can be wiped or sprayed in the same way that solvent-based stains can.

However, because waterborne products, particularly water-soluble dyes, dry quickly, you must move quickly when wiping them on. To avoid lap marks, apply a full, wet coat to the surface.

I usually get a good finish after two coats of top coat. I'd recommend three or more coats for added durability, such as on a tabletop.

While waterborne finishes do not emit the noxious fumes that solvent-based finishes do, they do emit some vapors. As a result, I take precautions.

I could use some cross ventilation while brushing finishes. I wear a respirator with organic vapor filters and ventilate the work area while spraying. Choose a synthetic bristle brush for finishing because natural bristles absorb water in waterborne products and begin to splay and lose their shape.

Synthetic bristles will not work. When applying a finish, keep the brush wet and avoid scraping the bristles against the can's edge. Allow any excess material to fall back into the compressor. This takes a little longer, but it prevents foaming. Then, in a thin coat, apply the material to the workpiece. If you apply it too thickly, it will run and sag.

To avoid lap marks, always work quickly and from a wet edge. The more you brush the finish, the more likely it is that it will foam and bubble. If you involve foaming, if one is available, add a flow additive for the finish. If not, as a last resort, try finishing with a few drops of lacquer thinner, mineral spirits, or milk.

These additives can reduce the finish's surface tension and improve flow. Waterborne materials can also be worked with using disposable foam or sponge brushes and paint pads. Use quick, light passes to apply the finish to the surface. The best results are obtained by spraying. A spray gun allows you to apply a complete, even coat to an entire piece in minutes. The finish dries so quickly that you can usually apply several coats in one day.

Waterborne finishes, because they contain a higher percentage of solids than most other finishes, have a tendency to run or sag if applied too heavily.

When spraying, apply just enough material to leave a shiny, wet sheen on the wood's surface, but not so much that it begins to run.

If you catch a run or drip while it is still wet, wipe it away with a clean, lint-free cloth and immediately recoat the area. Otherwise, sand and recoat any dried or skinned-over trouble spots with a razor blade. Spray tools made of plastic or stainless steel are ideal for use with waterborne products because they will not rust.

However, if your gun is made of corrosive metals, you can prevent rust by thoroughly drying it after use by blowing compressed air through it.

You can also remove any remaining water from the gun by passing a few ounces of denatured alcohol through it. When it comes to applying finishes, the cooperation of nature can certainly make a difference.

On dry, warm days, waterborne materials flow out smoothly, level quickly, and dry in less than an hour, sometimes in a matter of minutes when spraying.

You can apply several coats in one day if the temperature is around 70°F and the relative humidity is between 35 and 50%. However, if your finishing room is cold or the humidity is high, waterborne products can become irritable.

When waterborne goods are cold, they do not atomize properly, do not flow out well, and take longer to dry than usual. You should ideally heat your finishing room.

But there is another option. I've discovered that if I heat the finish to about 75° right before using it, I can apply top coats in a 45° room. I simply immerse the can of finish in a sink or bucket of hot water for a few minutes.

Never heat any type of finish material over an open flame or on a stove. The warm finish is simple to spray, flows well, and dries quickly. It can be more difficult to reduce humidity. A dehumidifier can reduce moisture content in a small room. However, if you have a shop near the sea, the tools can reduce humidity.

I've discovered that using a fan to blow warm air over the piece being worked on can help to mitigate the negative effects of high humidity.

Waterborne top coats, like other top coats, can be rubbed out to change the sheen. Just remember to stay away from steel. Wool can cause black spots and rust if pieces of it become lodged in the finish.

CHAPTER SEVEN

APPLYING WATER-BASED FINISHES

Many woodworkers avoid water-based finishes because they believe they cause excessive grain raising, do not adhere well over oil-based stains and look like plastic.

When I first started using water-based finishes, these items were difficult to use and didn't look so great. That is no longer the case. Water-based finishes are improving all the time. They also do not emit noxious fumes, are fast and are not flammable.

A survey of 25 water-based finishes was conducted. Manufacturers have been hard at work, and there is a slew of new finishes on the market. I tested nine new finishes and compared them to two tried-and-true finishes: nitrocellulose lacquer and shellac.

I also compared the new finishes to Camwood Super Lac, a water-based finish that performed admirably in the previous test especially when it comes to appearance.

When it comes to stain resistance, the new finishes shine. The majority were bulletproof. Grain raising was no longer an issue with the majority of the finishes, and some barely raised the grain at all.

Some of the finishes were difficult to apply, while the majority went on smoothly. The most subjective test, but a critical one, is rating the merchandise on appearance, and several finishes scored very high. Even the finishes with low appearance scores are light years ahead superior to what I was using a few years ago Water-based finishes are improving, and I believe the trend will continue.

Lacquer and shellac are traditional finishes with few ingredients, mostly resins (solids that form the finished film) and water. Solvents, also known as carriers, are substances that dissolve resins.

Water-based finishes, like oil-based finishes, contain resins and solvents. However, water-based finishes contain many more additives than traditional lacquers, some as many as 20, to compensate for the basic inconsistency of water and resin.

Other compounds, particularly those known as surfactants, allow water and resins to mix and form an emulsion. Alcohols or solvents frequently evaporate with the water, allowing the resins to coalesce and form the finished film.

While manufacturers are reluctant to divulge trade secrets, they did tell me that they have made progress with the types of resins and additives used in finishes. These advancements result in finishes that bond better to solvent-based products and are tougher while remaining easier to sand and rub.

The resins in the water-based finishes I tested are acrylic, urethane, or a combination of the two, except for one water-based shellac. Lacquer, for example, is one of the descriptive terms for these finishes. Most water-based finishes are technically lacquers, which means they can be lacquered, rather than polyurethane or varnish their solvents redissolved them.

To test all of the finishes, I cut squares from the same sheet of mahogany plywood. First, I stained half of each panel with Minmax red-mahogany oil-based stain.

I let the stain dry for two days before applying three coats of finish to each panel, using a brush, a spray gun, or a combination of the two, according to the manufacturer's recommendations.

I wait at least two hours between coats before lightly sanding and applying another. While some manufacturers sell sanding sealers, all of the products I tested can be used on bare wood, which is exactly what I did.

The panels were then subjected to common household compounds to see how they would fare. I sanded the top coats with 240-grit, 400-grit, and 600-grit sandpaper after finishing the various tests then rubbed them with pumice and rottenstone.

For comparison, I also tested traditional shellac, nitrocellulose lacquer, and a previously tested water-based product.

The adhesion test determines whether or not a water-based finish will adhere to an oil-based stain. I cut an X into the finish and it was applied over the stain with a sharp knife or razor.

Then I pressed a piece of packing tape firmly against the X. I let the tape sit for about 5 minutes before removing it. The finish remained consistent across eight panels. Only one finish was chipped off, causing the test to fail.

For the stain test, I used common foods and gave each finish what I call the kitchen-table test. Tables are prone to food spills, and a good finish should withstand the assault as well as the chemicals used to clean up the mess.

On each panel, I placed a small amount of the following common household items: milk, orange juice, hot coffee, mustard, ketchup, red wine, grape jelly, vinegar, and olive oil.

After an hour, I wiped each spot clean and checked for damage. If there was no damage, the finish was worth two points. If the finish was slightly damaged, it received 1 point.

No points were awarded if the finish was severely stained, damaged, or eaten away. Every finish I tested received at least 19 points, and several received a perfect 22. The most harm was done by Windex and Fantastik. Hot pots, cups, and spoons are frequently placed on tables. I put a spoon in boiling water for a few minutes to recreate this scenario.

I removed the spoon after it had cooled. The finish passed the test if the spoon left no mark. If the spoon became stuck to the finish or left a dull mark, It didn't make an impression.

Water-based finishes are notorious for causing excessive grain rising and making sanding difficult. Brushing a finger across the first coat after it has dried is a simple way to determine the roughness.

The first coat of finish is responsible for the majority, if not all, of the grain raising. In my test, I rated raised grain as heavy if a panel felt rough, like medium grit sandpaper.

I would have given the panel a moderate rating if it felt more like fine sandpaper. I rated it as minor if it felt like very fine sandpaper. I sanded all three coats with varying grits of fresh paper to determine whether a finish was easy or difficult to sand.

I considered not only how easily the finish powdered up and how much it clogged the paper, but also how hard I had to work to achieve a smooth, flat surface.

Fortunately, all of the finishes I tested were in the easy-to-moderate category. Indeed, several of the finishes were as easy to sand as lacquer and shellac.

I discovered that using 1,000-grit and 1,200-grit wet abrasive paper before rubbing out with pumice and rottenstone produced the best results for a high-gloss, rubbed-out finish.

Because the majority of the finishes performed well in the kitchen-table tests, the deciding factor is appearance. This is, of course, subjective. Something that appeals to me may not appeal to you.

To give a fair assessment, I showed the panels to a couple of other professional woodworkers and weighed their thoughts against mine. I used solvent-based lacquer as the standard against which I judged the appearance of all the finishes.

Lacquer gives the wood a warm tone, what I call a light amcolorlour, and the finish has clarity, which adds depth, especially in darker woods after three or more coats Finishes were downgraded if they had a cool or blue cast and were dull or cloudy.

Except for Cool-Lac, I would consider using any of these products if the color of the color war was not an issue. While the Cool-Lac performed well in the tests, even outperforming traditional shellac in terms of color I found the color to apply.

The product is very thin, has almost the consistency of water, and contains very few solids. As a result, the coats are thin and do not build well.

A deep, protective finish requires at least a half-dozen coats. Compliant Spray Systems Enduro Wat-R-Base Poly Overprint and Target Enterprises Oxford Hybrid Gloss Varnish are two of my favorite finishes. Enduro and Oxford have a similar appearance to solvent-based lacquer.

Because of their clarity, they give wood a warm tone and highlight the grain. Both are simple to apply, but the Enduro only requires three coats to achieve a good build.

I cut through to bare wood when I went to rub out the Oxford after three coats. If you want to rub this finish out to a high gloss, you'll need at least five coats.

If I had to choose between the two, I'd go with the Enduro because it dries so quickly and passed the adhesion test. Most people would struggle to tell the difference between Enduro and solvent-based lacquer.

The Oxford finish, which has a nice, warm tone like the Enduro, didn't adhere as well over an oil-based stain as it did over bare wood. This problem can be solved by using water or alcohol-based stain, or by applying a shellac sealer between the oil stain and the finish.

Not to be overlooked is Eclectic Merchandises Famo wood Super Lac, a finish that performed admirably in previous tests and ranks alongside the Enduro and Oxford. It is simple to use and apply.

It rubs out very well, has good depth, and has a color that is very similar to nitrocellulose lacquer.

Although some water-based products have improved to the point where they look like traditional lacquer or shellac right out of the can, others still have a long way to go.

Some appear bland, while others have a slight bluish cast. If you like everything about your finish except the color, think about toning the wood or the finish. Some finish manufacturers tone their products for customers who prefer a warm appearance. An additive in the Enduro Water Base Poly Overprint gives the finish a slight amber tone.

Hydrocode provides an amber additive for use in its finishes. Other products are available to assist you in coloring top coats. Whatever you do, don't go beyond what the manufacturer recommends for the finish.

Using shellac as a first or sealer coat will give the wood a warm glow. Additionally, it will raise and stiffen the grain, making it easier to sand.

Dewaxed fresh-blended shellac is recommended. You can also use dyes to color the wood. A thin coat of a highly diluted water-soluble dye should add just the right amount of color tour to the wood.

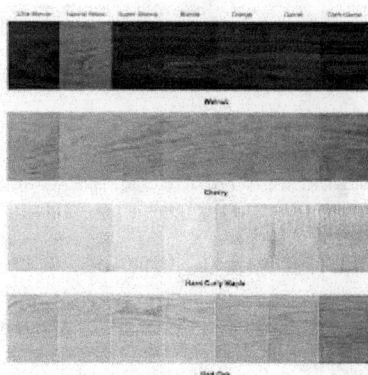

In reality, you are using the finish as a toner, which can be tricky. Pigments should be used sparingly: To change the appearance of a clear finish, you can use universal tinting colors, or UTCs, which are available at paint stores.

A small amount of an earthy tone, such as burnt umber or raw sienna, goes a long way toward adding color and warmth to an otherwise flat finish.

However, because pigments are dense, the finish may appear dark, cloudy, or muddy. When coloring a clear coat with pigments, use them sparingly and take great care to apply the finish as evenly as possible.

Dewaxed shellac can be used as a sealer coat on bare wood to add warmth to a finish. To change the tone of a finish, you can add universal tinting color or dissolved dye directly to it. Water-soluble dyes are preferable: Water-soluble dyes are a better alternative to pigments. First, dissolve a small amount of dye in water before adding a few drops at a time to the finish until the color is correct.

Keep in mind that water will thin the finish, so use it sparingly. Because dyes are transparent, they will not give the finish a muddy appearance.

Dyes, on the other hand, do not penetrate the resins; they only color the liquid part of the finish, which evaporates, leaving the dye in place.

This may result in some blotching. Alcohol dyes are the most effective way to tint finishes: dissolved dyes in alcohol will penetrate the resins in a finish and change their color colonized products have consistent tone color I like to use Homestead Finishing Merchandise's Trans Tint honey amber, which comes in concentrated liquid form. To achieve a warm tone, start with four to six drops per quart of finish.

Chapter Eight

Sanding Techniques

When I tell other woodworkers that sanding is one of my favorite activities, they are usually taken aback. But the truth is that I enjoy sanding, especially the final hand-sanding that indicates I've finished another job.

Sanding doesn't have to be a chore if you plan ahead of time and use the right tools. Sanding is done in two stages for me: shaping and smoothing. If the piece still requires shaping after being cut and pared with other tools, sanding tools can help.

If I'm working on a curved piece with changing grain direction, for example, a sanding tool will shape it more easily than an edge tool. There is also less risk of tearing the grain out.

Shaping is done with sandpaper ranging from SO-grit to 120-grit and powerful tools. I use a 4-inch by 24-inch belt sander, 5-inch and 5-inch rotary disc sanders, a right-angle random-orbit sander, an inflatable, handheld drum sander, and a spindle sander, depending on the job.

During shaping, I sand until there are no more machine marks, lumps, glue marks, or deep scratches visible. If I come across any rough patches, I go back to shaping with 100-grit sandpaper before smoothing.

Smoothing is typically accomplished with less aggressive machines and paper grits of 120 and finer. I use an orbital sander, palm and pistol grip random-orbit sanders, and various shapes and sizes of flexible and rigid hand sanding blocks.

This may appear to be a plethora of sanding tools. It all comes down to the fact that different tools are required to handle different jobs efficiently.

Both sanding stages should be completed as soon as possible—ideally, before assembly. This usually prevents me from standing for periods and from sanding into tight spots. A drawer is a useful tool.

Example
If the interior of a drawer needs to be sanded, do so before assembling the drawer. Sanding can be completed in minutes without the difficulty of sanding into inside corners.

Any miters or frame-and-panel assemblies can be handled in the same manner, which saves countless hours of frustration. After that, only a light hand-sanding is usually required before the finish is applied.

Sanding is the process of removing all machine marks and scratches left by rougher-grit sandpaper. The scratches from the previous sandpaper are then reduced using finer and finer grits until the piece is smooth. During the sanding process, grains frequently come off the paper.

Furthermore, if larger sanding grains from previous grits remain on the surface, they can be rubbed into the board and go into getting the wood. You can avoid this by vacuuming and sanding debris before progressing to finer grits.

My belt sander is the first tool I reach for on most projects. I've heard countless horror stories from students and woodworkers about belt sanders destroying projects, but with a few adjustments and practice, it's an invaluable tool.

One significant issue I've noticed is that the stock sheet metal plates on most belt sanders are rarely flat from the start, let alone after hours of use.

The metal distorts as the belt rubs against and heats the platen, resulting in a convex platen with a dished-out sanding pattern.

Fortunately, platens can be replaced with graphite-coated canvas, the same material used on larger sanding tools. The canvas can be purchased from Klingspor. To do its job, a belt sander must sit flat on the surface.

Begin by resting the sander on the work. When you pull the trigger, the machine will accelerate slightly. However, once it begins to sand, simply let it float on the surface.

Keep it moving, but don't grip the handles so tightly that it tilts or stops floating across the surface. Practices helps. Cover a surface with pencil marks to see if you're sanding where you think you're sanding.

Then, between inspections, sand for only a few seconds. You may be surprised to discover that you did not sand where you thought you did or vice versa. To sand ao the edge, the sander must hang about half its length over the edge.

If you're fed up with your belt sander, try a sanding frame. A frame aids in the control of a portable belt sander, allowing it to sand evenly.
Most sander manufacturers now sell sanding frames, and while the investment is small, the difference is enormous, especially if you're just starting.

The first step toward efficient sanding is to ensure that all scratches from the previous tool are removed. I work more with the coarser grits and less with the finer grits.

No single grit takes a long time if you sand thoroughly with each grit and move from one grit to the next without skipping. Don't skip the 120 and 150 grits after removing milling marks with 100 grit.

Regardless of how long you sand, 180-grit paper will not remove scratches caused by 100-grit paper. When sanding, sand the entire project one grit at a time.

Sanding only a portion of the venture will result in a poorly sanded venture. On rougher, more aggressive tools, use finer-grit sandpaper. I rarely use grits as coarse as 80 on my belt, orbital, or disc sanders. One hundred grit is nearly as fast but does not leave such deep scratches.

Remember that even though the grit on 100-grit paper is finer than on 80-grit paper, there is more of it, so the cutting speed is frequently the same.

The harder the wood, the more difficult it is to remove scratches. It is extremely difficult to remove scratches left by using rougher grits such as 80 or even 100 on woods such as hard maple. Start with 120-grit or finer paper to avoid this problem.

The majority of woodworkers simply let the tool do the work. This is especially true when it comes to sanding.

The power should come from the machine. The cutting action should be provided by sandpaper. The operator should only provide guidance, not downward pressure.

If you're getting tired from applying so much downward pressure, it's probably because your sandpaper is too dull or your machine is too light for the job.

An orbital sander is a fantastic tool, but if used incorrectly, it can quickly ruin a good project. The large 8-in. disc, a tool long used in the boatbuilding industry, will remove material at an incredible rate.
An orbital sander removes material by spinning the disc in a circular pattern. There are soft, hard, flat, and curved pads, which are all used for different techniques and jobs.

Soft pads conform to curved surfaces, and curved pads sand to perfection.

A delicate edge Surfaces are sanded flat with hard, flat pads. I use a Milwaukee variable-speed drill with pressure-sensitive adhesive foam.

I also recall that, while the grit on 100-grit paper is finer than on 80-grit paper, there is more of it, so the cutting speed is frequently the same.
The harder the wood, the more difficult it is to remove scratches. It is extremely difficult to remove scratches left by using rougher grits such as 80 or even 100 on woods such as hard maple.

Start with 120-grit or finer paper to avoid this problem.

"Let the tool do the work," as most woodworkers have heard. This is especially true when it comes to sanding.

The power should come from the machine. The cutting action should be provided by sandpaper. The operator should only provide guidance, not downward pressure.

If you're getting tired from applying so much downward pressure, it's probably because your sandpaper is too dull or your machine is too light for the job.

A random-orbit sander works similarly to an orbital sander, except that the disc rotates as well as orbits. The random action creates a sanding pattern on the wood's surface that is almost imperceptible. On flat surfaces, this can eliminate the need for hand sanding.

However, if you try to sand a curved surface or the edge of a venture, the sanding pad's rotation stops.

Sanding anything other than flat surfaces with a random orbit sander defeats the purpose of the machine.

CHAPTER NINE

HAND-SANDING TECHNIQUES

When hand-sanding a flat surface, always use a block. Hand-sanding without a block applies pressure only where your fingers are, resulting in a surface that will never be as flat as you'd like.

A block evenly distributes pressure across the board. Cushion the block with cork or felt to apply pressure to the high spots on the board without loading up the paper.

The dust is deposited more evenly on the surface as the sandpaper cuts, rather than just in a few spots. When hand-sanding, avoid using a hard wooden block. The sandpaper almost immediately fills up in a few places.

These spots then accumulate into small, volcano-shaped high points, resulting in a venture with scratches even after all of your hard work. My sanding block is simply a block of wood with felt glued to one side.

I cut a block the appropriate size, glued 8-in. thick felt to it, and that's all there is to it. I cut my sanding blocks to be one-third the size of a half-sheet of paper, then glue on the felt.

I tear sandpaper sheets in half, then fold this half piece into thirds. This system makes use of the entire sheet. Sand is exposed on two sides when folded in thirds.

One has ide grains of sand, while the other sticks to the left against the block. Refold the paper when both of these sides are worn to expose the last third for the final sanding.

This is one instance where saving labor is more valuable than saving material. I only use light pressure and frequently change the paper. When a piece of paper becomes dull, I discard it and replace it. A larger piece of sandpaper fits my hands better when hand-sanding contours. The diagrams below demonstrate how to use an entire sheet of sandpaper without wasting it.

1.   The sandpaper is creased but only torn halfway down its length.
2.   Fold the first quarter of the paper with the grit facing out.
3.   Fold the two sandpaper thicknesses onto the sheet's third quarter.
4.   The fourth quarter of the paper is folded into the final shape without ever folding grit onto grit.

The microscopic sand grains on sandpaper are initially extremely sharp. They cut easily into the surface with little effort or pressure.

Regardless, they quickly become dull. Sharp points break off, the paper becomes clogged with dust, and cutting is no longer possible—only rubbing. And the rubbing has the effect of polishing or glazing the surface of the wood rather than smoothing it. Sanding efficiently entails using a large amount of sandpaper.

It's a difficult rule to follow, but throwing away sandpaper before it becomes dull saves me a lot of time and sweat.

When sanding becomes easier, you can feel the paper lose its cutting action. This is because the paper is sliding across the surface rather than digging in. Use the oldest belt or disc until it becomes dull, then discard it and reach for a new one. You won't have 50 partially used sanding belts on the shelf this way.

Glue shadows may not be visible until the finish is applied, so sand a little more around glue joints to ensure that the glue is completely removed.

I always try to err on the side of too much sanding rather than too little. When you think you're finished, and a little more? If you're using a penetrating oil finish, the surface should be as smooth as possible, up to 400 grits.

If you're using water or alcohol-based stain, the stain will raise the grain when applied, so stopping at 150 or 220 grit is a better option. The surface will harden and stabilize after the first coat of finish sealer, paste filler, stain, or primer.

Then progress to finer grits, ranging from 180 to 400. Before you begin sanding, read and follow the instructions that came with the finishing materials.

Allow the tools and sandpaper to do their jobs. Your project will be perfectly sanded and ready for finishing in no time.

CHAPTER TEN

TABLE TOP FLATTENING

Flattening a tabletop is one of the most difficult sanding jobs, especially if your glued-up boards are not perfectly flush. However, the strategy is straightforward: eliminate the high spots while avoiding sanding the low spots. Here's the simplest way I've found to flatten a tabletop.

Step 1

Focus first on the glue joints, as they will eventually be the low point to which you must work once, they're flush. I sand with 100-grit belt sanders at a 45-degree angle, first to the right and then to the left of the grain pattern. Sand in both directions evenly. The sanding marks now have a chevron pattern.

Step 2

Make a batten out of a straight board and coat it in chalk to see where the top is not flat. Rubbing the board across the top quickly highlights the high spots that need more sanding.

Step 3

After removing all of the chalk, repeat the procedure. The piece will eventually be flat. This is not an oversimplification.

Once the surface is glands and the grain with the same grit to remove the cross-grain scratches. The same flattening technique can be used with a well-tuned and very sharp hand plane, but you risk digging into the work or causing tea rout.

A commercial drum sander, on the other hand, can flatten your tabletop in minutes for a few dollars.

Chapter Eleven

Creating a Curve

Fairing a curve is the process of shaping it to remove any lumps or hollows. In woodworking, as in sculpture, the only way to make the curve even is to remove material.

This means you should focus on the high points and ignore the low points. This sounds simple enough, but in practice, it can be difficult to tell the difference.

Sanding for the sake of sanding almost always results in a lumpier curve. Other woodworkers frequently attempt to smooth or fair a curved piece on the spindle sander by running the entire curve over the sander without stopping to feel the surface.

I know they're about to create a bigger problem than they already have, so I stop them and remind them that sanding done sparingly and selectively will give them the desired result.

The proper method is to sand the curve for only a few seconds, just long enough to remove tool marks. Then, with your fingers, run them over the surface to check for consistency. When you find a high spot, mark it with chalk or pencil and remove only those lumps, avoiding hollows as much as possible.

Stop and feel the surface again, marking the sanding spots as before. Gradually, the surface smooths out and the curve becomes more even.

On larger curves, the lumps can be difficult to detect at times. You can find high spots by applying chalk to a batten (a flexible piece of wood).

Rub this batten back and forth across the surface. The chalk will rub off on the high points, leaving a distinct area to sand.

Chapter Twelve

Spray-Finish Plunge

My first business was in a small garage. What little space I had was taken up by tools that were necessary for making furniture. A dust collector and a finishing room were left out.

As a result, obtaining dust-free finishes was difficult. Brushing on shellac and varnish was fine for small projects, but as I took on larger jobs and built more pieces, I switched to wipe-on oils because they were less fussy to apply.

Finally, I needed tougher finishes that were quick to apply. The solution was a spray system. Finishing with a spray is quick and simple. Brushes and rags are useless in some situations.

Spray finishes also look fantastic. The coating is more uniform, and the finishes are more consistent between pieces. But once I decided to go with spray finishes, I knew I needed to do some research.

Over the last ten years, the variety of spray systems has grown dramatically. Manufacturers have released small, low-cost units that are ideal for hobbyists and small businesses.

Furthermore, numerous advancements have been made in high-volume, low-pressure spray systems, or HVLP, particularly in terms of transfer.

An entry-level HVLP spray system costs around $200, and systems ranging from $200 to $500 are available.

These spray systems are not significantly more expensive than many power tools. Waterborne finishes have also improved, which has reduced the need for hazardous, solvent-based finishes.

Because water-based finishes are nonflammable, you no longer need a spray booth to get started. A clean spray area, a respirator, and adequate ventilation are all that are required. A spray system will also not leave you with a pile of oily rags that could catch fire.

I only brushed on varnishes for a few seconds. The varnish was just too slow to brush and dry, and I needed good lighting to brush, sand, and rub out the varnish.

For a while, I relied on wipe-on oils. I didn't need any special tools to oil, and I could oil even in less-than-ideal conditions. Because I wasn't creating a thick surface film like a varnish, I was less concerned about dust and lint becoming trapped in the film.

Oil finishes quickly became an important part of my marketing strategy as well. The majority of my customers prefer authentic, hand-rubbed finishes.

There are some disadvantages to oil finishing. An oil finish provides little protection, and it requires more maintenance than other top coats. Surface flaws, such as scratches, stand out more than they would with a film finish.

Oil finishes are also time and labor-intensive. An oil finish can take several days to apply depending on the temperature and humidity. It also necessitates a substantial amount of effort. It's difficult to get excited about rubbing multiple coats of oil of 400 wooden clock frames.

Spray finishing, as appealing as it is, has a few flaws. Setting up a secure, efficient system takes time and money. Aside from the gun, you'll need an air source, hoses, filters, and connectors.

Because spraying emits a finished mist into the air, you'll also need a spray area with good air circulation. Before you set up a booth to spray solvent-based finishes, check with your local building inspector.

However, if you only spray water-based merchandise, you won't need explosion-proof fans and fixtures. Spray finishes, unlike most brush-on and wipe-on finishes, must be filtered and then thinned to the proper viscosity.

Too thinner inner can cause lumpy finishes and orange peel, while too much thinner can cause drips and sags on vertical surfaces. It will also take longer to build to the proper film thickness.

As a result, you won't be able to get nice, glossy clear coats, and paints won't be able to hide the underlying surface or provide gcolorlodepth color much thinner and also extend the drying time, causing dust to accumulate.

Finally, it is critical to keep your spray gun clean. While cleaning does require some effort and time, cleaning a spray gun does not take any longer than cleaning a brush.

While some finish is wasted due to overspray, you can still reduce your material costs. I've had to reject far fewer spray-finished pieces than a brush or rag-finished pieces.

Spraying also saves money on labor. I more than covered the cost of the tools in the first month. My shop could no longer function without a spray system.

Chapter Thirteen
Spraying Advantages

1.   Spray finishes are easy to work with. Small scratches and marks are better hidden under a sprayed translucent finish than under an oil finish because a sprayed finish is built up in thin layers. Surface prep is still essential. This is especially true when spraying paints or stains that are opaque.

2.   Spray finishes dry quickly. In an hour, you can spray 30 stools or 1,000 small wooden blocks. Because the sprayer breaks down the finish into small particles, each coat dries quickly. Several varnishes, water-based products, and sprayed lacquers are touch dry in minutes. Some can be sanded and recoated in a matter of hours. The dust has a limited time to settle on the work while the coat is tacky, reducing the need for sanding between coats.

3.   Spray finishes are adaptable. Any finish that can be applied. Spraying can be done with a brush or a rag. You can spray shellac, lacquer, and other solvent-based products if you use explosion-proof booth materials. You can still spray water-based finishes if you don't have a booth. Water-based contact cement, which works well for laminate work, can be applied with some spray systems.

4.   Spray finishes can be controlled precisely. Spray-gun adjustments, combined with proper spray techniques, give you excellent control over how and where the finish is applied. A brush transfers nearly 100% of the finish to the work, but you must be careful to keep the coat even and at the proper thickness.

Even though a spray gun's transfer efficiency is lower than that of a brush, ranging between 65 and 85 percent, you can adjust air pressure, fan size, and fluid flow to ensure light and even coats. There are no brush or lap marks because the atomized material flows together uniformly.

5.   Spray finishes are simple to apply. Spray finishing is a simple process. In less time than it takes to master brushing or wiping on a finish, you can learn how to spray a simple case or frame. Spray stains and dyes to achieve uniform coverage and color depth with lit practice e you can use tinted clear finishes to create special effects like shading or sunbursts. Because spraying allows for a wider range of finishes, your ventures will appear more professional.

6.   The quality of spray finishes is consistent. The overall higher quality of finish that you can achieve is without a doubt the best reason for investing in a spray system. Spray-on finishes outperform brush-on and wipe-on finishes. Spray tools reduce the problems caused by brushing, such as runs, drips, and air bubbles. And the brush strokes are gone. Light, even coats of finish can be applied to an entire piece, regardless of size or shape.

When you mention the names Delta, General, or Powermatic to a group of cabinetmakers, everyone knows you're talking about woodworking machinery.

Mention Devillis, Mattson, or Sharpe to the same group of people, and you'll most likely get blank stares. These are just three of the dozens of companies that manufacture spray-finishing tools.

Many woodworkers probably don't know as much about selecting a spray system as they do about purchasing a table saw.

Given that a high-quality spray system can cost as much as a good table saw, it pays to do your homework before purchasing. First, some knowledge of spray-gun anatomy would be beneficial.

Chapter Fourteen

How to use a Spray Gun

The basic operating principle of a spray gun is simple. A stream of liquid finish is forced into an airstream, where it is broken down into tiny droplets and carried to the target surface.

It may appear simple, but a collection of precision parts must be assembled. collaborate to pull the whole thing off Air flows from the compressor hose through a valve in a standard high-pressure system a series of valves and baffles in the gun's body and out through an air cap

The maximum atomization pressure at the air cap is controlled by the valves and baffles. The size and placement of the holes in the air cap determine the volume of air used by the gun as well as the spray pattern.

A standard air cap for furniture finishing produces a tapered pattern that measures 9 to 11 inches long. The gun typically consumes about 8 cubic feet per minute of air at 50 psi.

Pulling the trigger separates the needle from the fluid tip, allowing the finish to enter the airstream. The amount of material sprayed is determined by the size of the orifice and the viscosity of the finish.

I've discovered that the orifice is excellent for finishing furniture. Fluid tips and needles are available in matched sets. Most spray-system manufacturers have technical support departments that can help you choose the right one.

When the finish reaches the tip, high-pressure air from the air cap blasts the stream into tiny droplets. Droplets can range in size from 15 microns to 70 microns or more.

The size is determined by the fluid viscosity and the tools. The atomized finish flows together to form a smooth film after it is deposited. The smaller the droplets, in general, the better the finish.

A gun with an aluminum cup and fluid passages is suitable for finishing with hydrocarbon-solvent-based finishes such as nitrocellulose lacquer and oil-based varnish.

However, if the same gun is used to apply a finish that contains a chlorinated solvent, such as methylene chloride, which is the main ingredient in many paint strippers, it will be corroded beyond repair in a matter of hours. Aluminum parts will corrode even with non-flammable solvent cleaner.

Similarly, if the gun is not cleaned immediately after use, the alkaline component of waterborne finishes can damage bare aluminum parts.
Some low-cost units combine plastic cups and dip tubes with brass fluid handling parts as a corrosion-resistant alternative to aluminum.
However, brass corrodes quickly, especially if the gun is used to spray pigmented finishes such as paint.

The pigments function similarly to abrasives used in sandblasters. Mild-steel components, particularly fluid tips and needles, are also common in low-cost spray guns. While steel is compatible with the majority of finishes, it has a nasty rusting tendency.

One option is to purchase a gun with a stainless-steel cup and fluid handling parts, but these are expensive. These guns are appropriate for industrial users, but they are excessive for small shops.

Some spray guns, as an alternative, have stainless-steel fluid passages and a Teflon-lined aluminum cup. The Teflon coating protects the cup from corrosion and makes clean-up a breeze.

Chapter Fifteen

High-Pressure Spray Tools

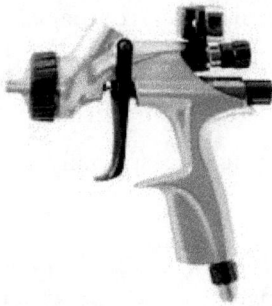

In response to the automotive industry's need for high-speed finishing, high-pressure spray tools were developed. Spray components haven't changed much since then.

A complete system is made up of three major components: a compressor with associated hoses, a tank, and pressure regulator, an oil and water separation device, and a spray gun.

The air compressor is the heart of the spray system; spray performance is affected by both horsepower and tank size. A 3-hp compressor with a 10-cfm air output and a 20-gallon air tank is the bare minimum.

Water vapor in the air condenses to form a liquid when compressed. The water that passes through the spray gun, if not eliminated, will cause a slew of finishing issues.

As a result, an oil and water separator is an essential component of any compressor-driven spray system. The separator also removes any remaining oil used to lubricate the compressor

There are two types of high-pressure spray guns: internal and external mix. The mix designation is determined by where the airstream enters the fluid stream.

The majority of internal mix guns produce a coarsely atomized spray. While not suitable for applying lacquers or other fast-drying finishes, this spray is ideal for applying thick, difficult-to-spray materials such as adhesives and pore fillers.

Internal-mix guns use little air and can be powered by a 1-hp or 2-hp compressor. However, they can only spray slow-drying varnishes and paints.

External-mix guns, on the other hand, are adaptable. They are the most commonly used spray guns in woodworking shops. Hundreds of fluid-tip/needle/air-cap combinations are available to spray virtually any liquid at virtually any pressure. When larger quantities are required, external mix guns can be fed from a 1-qt. siphon cup attached to the gun or pumped from a 1-gallon remote pressure pot.

There are two disadvantages to using external-mix spray guns. They use a lot of air, so they need at least a 3-hp compressor, preferably a 4-hp or 5-hp compressor. And they aren't very good at finishing the job.

Only about 35% of the finish hits the target; the rest is wasted as overspray. High-pressure spray guns are only useful in a shop with a good spray booth.

HVLP spray tools have been around for quite some time. Woodworkers used to paint models and birdhouses with HVLP painting attachments that came with canister vacuum cleaners in the late 1950s.

HVLP tools are becoming more sophisticated, but the underlying concept remains unchanged. HVLP systems use high volumes of air rather than high pressure to atomize the finish.

HVLP spray guns, as opposed to conventional spray guns, produce a soft spray pattern. The advantages include increased transfer efficiency, low overspray, and virtually no bounce-back. Simply put, HVLP spray guns finish the job while leaving less residue in the shop and on the environment. Spray-tool manufacturers have approached HVLP in two very different ways.

Some use advanced turbine-driven systems, while others use advanced conversion-air HVLP systems powered by a standard air compressor. Airless systems are more commonly associated with house painting than with furniture finishing. Airless spray systems, on the other hand, are common in large furniture factories.

Pressures approaching 4,000 psi are used in these commercial units. Nonetheless, high pressure, high delivery, and high efficiency are all present with a hefty price tag

Consumer-sized airless units are still available in stores. On certain projects, I like to use them to apply latex paint and oil-based varnish. The size of an airless gun's motor influences both its price and its versatility.

A 110-watt gun has enough power to spray untinned latex paint. However, with a 45-watt unit, the paint must be significantly thinned. A motor rated at 85 watts or higher is usually sufficient for spraying furniture.

Regrettably, airless spray guns produce a coarse spray pattern. As a result, only slow-drying paints and varnishes should be used with them.

Lacquers, including waterborne varieties, tend to dry before the droplets combine. The result is a rough texture, similar to that of an orange peel.

Despite these limitations, an airless spray system can help you get started with spray finishing at a low cost.

One of the advantages of an airless spray unit is that it does not require a bulky air hose. It only requires an extension cord.

If you're looking for a spray system for your shop, consider conversion-air HVLP spray systems. You'll also have an air compressor to help you with other tasks around the house.

Chapter Sixteen

HVLP Spray Systems

Turbine HVLP systems use a fan similar to those found in vacuum cleaners to generate 45 to 110 cfm of air at pressures ranging from 2 to 7 psi. Turbines are available in three power levels: one, two, and stages gages ages Each stage of the turbine, or fan section, adds about 40 cm and 2 psi of air output.

A turbine, unlike a compressor, produces a continuous stream of warm, dry air at a constant pressure. Pressure regulators and air dryers or separators are no longer required. However, warm air can be an issue. Some spray guns' metal handles can become unbearably hot.

Furthermore, dried finish drops tend to accumulate on the fluid tip; eventually, the finish glob breaks free and deposits itself on the freshly sprayed surface.

On the plus side, turbine systems are small, easy to store and run on 110v power.

The greater the number of stages in a turbine, the wider the viscosity range of the spray finish. I had to thin the finish when spraying with a one-stage turbine to get proper atomization.

Thinning is the death knell for some waterborne finishes. When I used a two-stage turbine to spray the same finish, there was enough power to spray without thinning. I didn't try a three-stage turbine designed for multiple guns and high output because they're too expensive.

HVLP conversion-air spray systems
HVLP conversion-air systems pass compressed air at high pressure through a high volume of air at low pressure through the gun's baffles and expansion chambers

Conversion-air guns have a bad reputation for consuming a lot of air. However, the most recent conversion-air spray guns will work with most 3 or 4-hp compressors. If you already have a compressor in your shop, it could power a conversion-air HVLP gun.

Conversion-air systems have a significant advantage over turbines in that the atomization pressure at the air cap can be adjusted between 2 and 10 psi with most guns to accommodate a wide range of coating viscosities.

I side-by-side compared the two types of HVLP systems. The conversion-air system consistently produced a finer atomized finish, a faster delivery rate, and a significant reduction in overspray.

The hose and spray gun's quick-connect fittings must be matched, and connectors are available at most auto-paint and compressor repair shops. It was around 50 years ago that I purchased a new vacuum cleaner.

A crude, plastic spray-gun attachment was included in the box with the accessories.

The gun was attached to one end of the vacuum cleaner hose, which was also attached to the vacuum cleaner motor's blower.

For decades, the only tool on the market was high-pressure, compressor-driven spray tools. Spraying anything from water-thin liquids to molasses-thick paste, the tools are extremely versatile.

This versatility, however, comes at a cost: the spray gun must be tethered to a large, high-output, high-pressure compressor.

Furthermore, the transfer efficiency of these spray guns—a measure of how well the gun delivers the finish—is notoriously low.

SCAQMD and other air-quality agencies across the country enacted stringent regulations in the early 1980s requiring spray guns to have transfer efficiencies of 65 percent or higher while operating at air pressures of 10 psi or less.

High transfer efficiency and low overspray mean more coating on the venture and less in the air, which is better for the sprayer operator and the environment.

Companies developed two distinct spray-gun systems to comply with the new regulations.

High-pressure sprayer manufacturers, such as Banks and Devillis's, modified their basic high-pressure guns to create one that converts high-pressure, compressor-supplied air to low-pressure air at the air cap.

For obvious reasons, this type of gun is known as a conversion HVLP spray gun. Although the original conversion guns met all regulatory requirements, they were massive air hogs.

An 1O-hp compressor was required for just one spray gun, which consumed air at a rate of 20 cu. ft. per minute or higher. Large shops could accommodate conversion guns, but small, custom shops lacked the necessary air power.

The turbine HVLP spray gun was created to meet this market demand. A small, high-output blower (the turbine) supplies a large volume of low-pressure warm air through a fairly large-diameter hose in this system.

Because each component-turbine, hose, and spray gun plays an important role in overall performance, turbine HVLP sprayers are sold as a system rather than as individual components.

These small, self-contained, portable spray systems are becoming increasingly popular among woodworkers, especially as prices continue to fall.

Most stores will let you try out an HVLP sprayer before you buy it. Here are six things to keep an eye out for:

1. Use an inexpensive pressure gauge to check the atomization pressure at the spray gun's tip: Spraying requires a minimum of 2 psi. The majority of them succeed.

2. Check the air-hose flexibility while the turbine is running and the gun is attached. You should be able to maneuver the gun into tight spaces without straining your arm or tripping over the hose.

3. Remove the gun and measure the air temperature at the hose's end. Temperatures above 120°F tend to clog the nozzle and air cap, particularly with water-based finishes.

4. Examine the spray-gun air cap. It should have smooth surfaces and clean air holes.

5. Smell the air coming out of the gun. Plasticizer vapors used in the manufacture of the air hose may be irritating.

6. Examine the spray-gun cup for corrosion; do not purchase a corroded cup.

In HVLP jargon, a turbine is a fancy term for a vacuum cleaner motor. The majority of HVLP systems developed in North America are powered by Ametek Lamb Electric Co. motors.

Small, high-speed compression fans are driven by the motors. Turbines are classified according to the number of fans called stages attached to the central motor shaft. One fan is used in single-stage turbines, two fans in two-stage turbines, and so on.

More stages equate to more airflow and pressure at the spray gun. You might think that comparing the turbine power of different HVLP systems is a good idea based on airflow figures, but this is not always the case.

I found the manufacturer's air-output ratings to be practically useless for comparison purposes. The air output of the Apollo 700, a two-stage unit, for example, is the output of the Lemmer T55, another two-stage unit, is rated at 112 cfm, while the output of the Lemmer T55 is rated at 55 cfm.

The Amptek Lamb data sheets indicate that the outputs should be nearly identical. I spoke with an airflow engineer to learn how to calculate accurate airflow values.

Following this advice, I built a test chamber out of a 6-foot section of a 6-inch-diameter heating duct and conducted MN airflow tests.
I borrowed a hot-wire anemometer, which is used to measure airflow, and measured the air output of each HVLP turbine at the end of the air hose and the spray gun's air cap.

The outcomes surprised me. Apollo's air-output values dropped by 80 percent, to 23 cm, according to my measurements end of the hose and 11 cfm measured at the spray gun

However, the Apollo unit was not alone. I concluded that all of the manufacturers in this test grossly overstated the air output of their respective turbines.

Air-output figures published in manufacturer literature are clearly of little value to the consumer. Fortunately, airflow figures aren't as important as atomization pressure, which is the true key to successful spray finishing.

To compare turbine HVLP spray systems, the best measurement is the atomization pressure at the spray gun. Best of all, you can test it out before putting your money on the line.

All you need is a pressure gauge that can measure from 0 to 10 psi. I bought a fuel-pump gauge from an auto parts store and used it to measure the air pressure at the supply hose's end and the atomization pressure at the spray gun's air cap.

I discovered yet another lack of correlation between my measured pressures and the manufacturers' published atomization pressures. My figures on regular were roughly one-third less than those claimed by each manufacturer.

Lemmer was a notable omission, as it understated the atomization pressure on its model T-55 gun by about a third. The difference between 4.25 psi and 2.8 psi may not appear to be significant, but it makes a significant difference in gun performance.

To put these figures in context, you can spray an undiluted conversion varnish at 4 psi but not at 2.8 psi. A typical HVLP turbine's fans spin at around 20,000 revolutions per minute.

That much speed produces a lot of heat, which warms the air supply to the gun. Warm air, as far as I can tell, is more of a bother than a benefit.

Some manufacturers claim that the heat aids in the flow of the finish, but I doubt the finish is in the airstream long enough to warm up significantly.

Nonetheless, the warm air heats the air cap and the fluid nozzle, causing them to dry out and eventually clog the gun with any overspray that may land on those parts.

This is not a serious spraying problem; rather, it is a clean-up problem, particularly on units that generate higher temperatures. Even so, if everything else were equal, I'd go for the cooler outfit. I used a dial thermometer to check the temperature after 10 minutes of operation.

Crush resistance and flexibility are two qualities I look for in an HVLP system's air supply hose. You will invariably step on the hose. A crushed hose will cut off the air supply at the gun while spraying.

My crush test revealed that all units passed with flying colors. Another issue is hose flexibility. A stiff hose makes it difficult to use the spray gun.

The maneuver, which could result in a poor spray job. Apollo connects the gun and the air-supply hose with a short length of highly flexible hose. This configuration provided the most maneuverability and made it the most comfortable sprayer to operate.

The Wagner unit has a heavy-duty rubber hose that offers nearly the same flexibility: In comparison, the hoses on the other three sprayers felt a little stiff.

Except for Wagner, all manufacturers offer plasticized vinyl sprayers attached to air hoses Vinyl hoses stiffen with age, especially at the high operating temperatures of these sprayers because vinyl emits plasticizers that allow it to be flexible

During normal operation, all of the vinyl hoses gave off an unpleasant odor to the fan.

During my air-output tests, the concentration of plasticizer vapors emitted by the Campbell Haus Feld unit was high enough to make my eyes water and breathing difficult.

I had to leave the shop and turn on a ventilation fan. The rubber hose on the Wagner, on the other hand, had no discernible odor. The insides of turbine-driven HVLP spray guns and conventional high-pressure spray guns are completely different.

The large air passages inside an HVLP gun make it more robust than a standard spray gun. I prefer the extra bulk because it fits my hand better. But that isn't the only distinction between the two designs. The fan-pattern adjustment knob found on high-pressure spray guns is absent from HVLP guns.

An HVLP gun's fan pattern is instead adjusted by moving the air cap in or out relative to the fluid nozzle.

Most HVLP guns, unlike high-pressure guns, are bleeder-type guns. Even when you're not spraying the finish, air flows or bleeds through the gun continuously. As a result, bleeder guns are inconvenient for me.

The constant flow of air stirs up dust in my shop, and the noise is bothersome. HVLP guns with no bleeder are powered by a turbine. Only high-priced industrial spray systems have stops when you release the trigger.

To my surprise, the Wagner 2600 system includes an industrial-quality, non bleeder gun as standard equipment. Thinner finishes require less atomization pressure than denser finishes, according to a fundamental principle of spray finishing.

You can greatly improve transfer efficiency and reduce overspray by keeping the pressure set to the minimum required to atomize a finish. Simply adjust the regulator on a compressor-driven sprayer to change the atomization pressure.

However, turbine-powered HVLP systems lack a pressure regulator. American Turbine, Campbell Haus Feld, and Wagner have addressed this issue by incorporating an air-reducer valve into their spray guns.

Closing the valve to reduce atomization pressure at the spray tip improves the performance of these guns to some extent, especially when spraying thin finishes.

With the five HVLP systems we looked at, I sprayed nearly 6 gal. of finish, which included polyurethane varnish, nitrocellulose lacquer, and a spray-grade water-based finish.

None of the units had any difficulties spraying any of the finishes. Nonetheless, some systems outperformed others. Wagner's low overspray and fine atomization pressure particularly impressed me.

The American Turbine AT 950 and Lemmer T-55 were both strong contenders for second place. I had trouble adjusting the needle-packing gland on the Apollo 700 spray gun, and I never got it perfectly adjusted.

Either the packing was too tight, preventing the needle from stopping the fluid flow, or it was too loose, allowing the finish to drip onto my skin hand.

Campbell Haus Feld created a coarse spray that left the visible orange peel on the sprayed surface. Because of a poor air-cap design, it also left heavy stripes in the finish.

Unfortunately, there are no standard test techniques for evaluating spray gun performance in the HVLP sprayer industry. Because each manufacturer develops its spray tests, comparing systems based on manufacturer claims is difficult.

I conducted a series of tests in my place to see how well these systems lived up to their claims of high transfer efficiency and low overspray.

HVLP sprayers are distinguished by their high transfer efficiency and low overspray. Some industrial sprayers claim to have a transfer efficiency of 90%. It is possible to achieve 90 percent transfer efficiency by spraying only the center of a large, flat panel, but few of us finish three-dimensional furniture in this manner.

To simulate a piece of furniture, I built three plywood boxes 24 in. long by 12 in. wide by 10 in. high for my tests. I calculated the transfer efficiency by weighing the spray gun and the boxes before and after each test.

I tested each HVLP unit three times before averaging the results to determine transfer efficiency. To be fair, I sprayed the same finish with each gun after adjusting each one to produce a 6-in. spray pattern.

The high transfer efficiency achieved by all of the units I tested surprised me. In anyone's book, 69 percent transfer efficiency is excellent. Overspray and atomization are more arbitrary measurements.

To different finishers, overspray means different things. Overspray, to me, is that small amount of finish that falls back onto the sprayed surface, giving the finished piece a rough texture.

To assess this elusive but critical parameter, I simply placed a grid over the test spray pattern and compared the number of squares inside the central spray pattern to the total number of squares with finish in them. A percentage was obtained by simple division.

While this test isn't perfect, the overspray values I calculated match what I saw in my spray booth. In most cases, an overspray of 20% or less is acceptable.

Based on my spraying experience with high-pressure and other HVLP systems, atomization is purely arbitrary. Fine atomization is comparable to that of a high-pressure gun; coarse atomization is incompatible with furniture finishing.

I compared the test sprayers to common high-pressure tools. I ran the same tests with my Sinks model 95 high-pressure spray gun. My trusty Sinks was the clear winner of the atomization contest, but it had a dismal 42 percent transfer efficiency and exorbitant overspray.

The air cap has a significant impact on transfer efficiency, overspray, and overall spray gun performance. A high-quality air cap will have clean, crisp holes in the air horns and a smooth, bump-free surface.

Chapter Seventeen

Vacuum Motor Spray Rig

For years, I used a traditional compressor-driven setup for spray finishing. I was never completely happy with the setup, so I recently built my own HVLP unit to replace it.

What bothers me about traditional spraying? To begin with, finishing the inside of a case while a swirling cloud of overspray billowed back in my face. I can't see what I'm doing, and no matter what mask I wear, I end up ingesting a large dose of compounds 110.

Overspray bothers me even when I'm spraying water-based finishes, which are inherently safer.

While neither toxic nor flammable, water-based finishes are expensive, so blasting these precious fluids all over the booth with air compressed to 50 pounds per square inch makes even less sense (psi).

HVLP spraying appeared to be the solution to these problems. This technique promised to transfer 70% to 80% of the material from the gun to the object, compared to 20% to 30% with a conventional setup.

HVLP guns have large hoses and air passages to accommodate a stream of warm, dry, low-velocity air. They use a lot of air—up to 30 cubic feet per minute (din)—but at only 5 psi.

I had a 3-hp compressor, so installing a large, low-pressure regulator to feed 5-psi air to the gun seemed simple. But there was a snag. A 3-hp piston compressor cannot continuously pump 30 efm at any pressure.

The rule of thumb is one horsepower for every four cubic feet of air, and we're talking about large, healthy industrial horses, not underfed home-improvement horses.

Because 8-hp to 10-hp compressors are expensive, connecting my small compressor to a tank the size of a submarine seemed like a bad idea.

I decided to look into the turbine compressors sold with HVLP guns because they seemed impractical. I borrowed an HVLP unit from a friend and finished some bathroom cabinets with it. It performed admirably, with almost no overspray, good atomization, and excellent fluid and pattern control. My only criticisms were that the hose was too long and that the gun's handle became too hot.

As I used the HVLP unit, I couldn't help but think that if it acts and sounds like a vacuum cleaner, it must be a vacuum cleaner. I took a peek inside. Inside was a two-stage vacuum cleaner turbine with an 8-amp motor. Later, I decided to construct my own HVLP turbine compressor. How did I do it? So, let's get started on it.

A centrifugal turbine compressor is used in an HVLP machine. It consists of a box with an inlet to bring air into the turbine and an outlet chamber to capture and route the compressed air discharged by the turbine to your sprayer hose.

Large vacuum cleaner turbines are integrated with their electric motors and are referred to as vacuum motors. First, purchase a vacuum motor. Visit an industrial supply company or request a catalog.

There are numerous options available, including bearing type, motor voltage, number of compressor stages, and motor amperage. The most important consideration for this application is to use bypass motor cooling rather than flow-through motor cooling.

This indicates that the motor is cooled by a separate fan. If the vacuum inlet or outlet is obstructed, the motor will not overheat.

Single-stage compressors move large amounts of air while producing the lowest pressure.

Two and three-stage units provide higher pressure air at a lower volume but typically have more powerful motors and, as a result, better overall performance.

I went with a two-stage turbine powered by a 13-amp motor rated at 116 cfm. I could have bought a less powerful unit, but I wanted to be able to use two spray guns on occasion, and I like heavy machinery.

You could try the Amptek for a one-gun setup. I spent less than $170 on the rest of the parts in my HVLP unit, including the hose but not the gun.

The turbine housing is clamped between two bulkheads using foam gaskets to mount these motors. First, construct the rear bulkhead. Cut it to size, then the band saw a circular hole and chamfer the back side.

The chamfer directs motor-cooling air away from the motor housing. Cut the positioning ring to size and use the jigsaw to rough out the hole, leaving it slightly undersized.

I cut the hole with a fly cutter on the drill press to make an exact-size Masonite routing template. To finish the hole in the positioning ring, I used the routing template.

Cut the housing sides, top, and bottom to size, and make the rear bulkhead dado in each. Then, in the side pieces, drill the cooling outlet holes.

Assemble the housing with the back bulkhead in place, then drop in the positioning ring and glue it in place. For the housing pieces, I used screwed butt joints and relied on the bulkhead to stiffen the box.

The turbine is held in place by the circular rabbet formed by the bulkhead and positioning ring, and it is separated from the wood by silicone rubber sealant.

Cut three 2-in. long pieces of soft rubber tubing that compress to about under moderate pressure, 8 in. Place the housing on its back and generously apply silicone to the rabbet. Push the turbine down into the wet silicone after laying the three pieces of tubing across the rabbet at 12 o'clock, 4 o'clock, and 8 o'clock.

If you want to remove the turbine later, spray the rim with an anti-stick cooking spray like PAM before inserting it into the silicone.

Allow the silicone to set before trimming the squeeze out and tubing ends. Next, route gasket grooves around the housing's front edge and press lengths of 8 in. soft rubber tubing into them.

Make the front and back covers, as well as the 11" by 11" rings. Glue the weatherstrip to the back and front, then screw it on. The filter's base is held in place by four short dowels, and a bracket pulls it tight against the cover.

Two threaded rods screwed into the front cover are joined by a hardwood crosspiece with a bolt through its center. A washer and wing nut secure the filter's closed end to the crosspiece. You could also experiment with a large automotive filter. In that case, a Masonite or plywood disc held against the front cover by a similar bracket could be used.

Install the electrical components, including a heavy-duty switch, a circuit breaker rated for your motor, and the power supply cord the rear cover Then adds rubber feet, a carrying handle, and a cord-management system.

I experimented with three different types of hose. All of them can be outfitted with standard garden hose threaded fittings or quick-connect couplers.

The lightweight, corrugated type included with most factory-built HVLP sprayers was the most adaptable, but its rough inner surface didn't deliver as much air as the smoother types.

A plastic garden hose is inexpensive, smooth on the inside, and flexible when warm, but when used, the heated air causes the hose to soften and kink easily.

Shields extra heavy-duty/FDA hose, which is available from marine distributors, is my personal favorite. It's made of soft, flexible vinyl that's been molded around a hard vinyl helix.

The manufacturer recommends it for use in boat plumbing below the water line, which means it can withstand a lot of heat as well as mechanical and chemical abuse.

I experimented with different locations for the outlet holes and found no discernible differences. However, I improved output by installing a fairing made of a strip of plastic laminate, which made the outlet chamber roughly cylindrical.

Drill one or two outlet holes in the housing, insert pipe thread close nipples and attach adapters to the nipples to provide male hose threads.

You can't just connect your old gun to your HVLP turbine for gun control. HVLP guns are designed to atomize fluids using low-pressure air. The list price for these guns is around $300.

My favorite of the HVLP guns I've tried is the Devillis's. The because the current model has stainless-steel fluid passages and a stainless-steel needle, water-based finishes will not corrode. And Much to my relief, the handle is a nylon composite that does not get hot when in use.

Chapter Eighteen

Touch-Up Guns

Some woodworkers are power tool addicts who collect routers. Others prefer hand tools and may have hundreds of planes and chisels at their disposal. I must admit that I have a spray gun addiction.

I used to have more than 14 in my collection, and I eventually sold most of them, but the collection has grown back into the double digits. A touch-up gun is the one I use the most out of all my spray guns.

The touch-up gun can do more than what its name suggests. I frequently use these little gems for finishing smaller projects, spraying stains, shading, and toning finishes, and touching up finishes that require minor repairs.

Because some of these guns are so cheap, I don't mind if I ruin one of them by accidentally leaving something in the gun that I shouldn't, such as milk paint or catalyzed lacquer.

I frequently apply stains in multiple layers. My favorite first stain color is a water-soluble dye stain, and I've discovered that a touch-up gun is the best applicator, especially on large pieces where brushing on a dye stain can cause lap marks.

Atomization isn't necessary for a simple dye stain, so I just use the gun to wet down the wood with dye and then blot up the excess. I can simply adjust the angle of the fan to hit the corners first for intricate inside areas.

I also reduced the amount of air used so that the vortex of the spray pattern did not prevent the dye from reaching tight corners.

A touch-up gun makes it simple to match sapwood to heartwood. You can reduce both the fan pattern and the amount of fluid used to create a subtle line of color that matches the sapwood to the heartwood.

When I do this, I usually begin by wetting down the entire area with the stain's solvent—alcohol, water, or mineral spirits—to get a better idea of the color I need to use.

After the base stain colors have been applied, shading and toning are usually applied. My favorite toner is made by combining dye with a finish to produce a translucent effect. It can be used for both general color applications and more specific shading applications.

Most standard-size guns and touch-up guns can be adjusted for the relatively wide fan pattern required to apply a toner, but shading is best done with a touch-up gun. The touch-up gun is your best finishing tool if you want to darken an edge molding or add a bit of dark color around the perimeter of a drawer or tabletop.

I rarely finish a piece of furniture without running into a problem, and one of the most common is rubbing through the finish and stain staining job is nearly finished.

You can draw some color or color the finish on a specific problem area if you have a gravity-feed gun with an airbrush attachment.

If you don't have this attachment for your regular spray gun, a touch-up gun's small spray pattern allows you to feather in finish or color so that it blends in seamlessly.

When I do this, I take a piece of cardboard that is several inches larger on all sides than the affected area and cut a slit down the middle with my table saw blade.
This mask is taped or held over the rubbed-through area, and I use my touch-up gun to apply the missing stain. I let it dry before applying a clear finish.

But, before that dry, I remove the mask and spray several coats of clear finish in the appropriate sheen with the gun set to a small setting.

pattern. After the repaired finish has dried completely, I can blend or feather in the finish with steel wool as needed.

Touch-up guns are smaller versions of regular spray guns, but they only come in two varieties: a siphon feesiphonr head tan rigger design, and a gravity-feed version.

Both styles are available in conventional air-driven or HVLP configurations, with the HVLP models being slightly more expensive.

The most expensive siphon-feed HVLP touch-up gun costs around $300, but a conventional air-driven, Taiwanese-made, overhead trigger gun can be had for less than $60.

The price range for gravity-feed models is roughly the same. Nonetheless, some gravity-feed models are available with airbrush bottle adapters, increasing the versatility of these guns, particularly for touch-up work.

Touch-up guns can be an invaluable asset in small businesses. They usually only need 4 to 5 cups. ft. of air per minute, which is a small amount of air that almost any compressor can handle.

Touch-up guns are also easy to maneuver in tight spaces and when finishing small items due to their smaller size. This is extremely useful when applying stain or a finish inside small cabinets.
When I first started spray finishing, I was blown away by how simple it was to lay down smooth, blemish-free top coats with any material imaginable. I was less thrilled with disassembling and cleaning the gun after each use.

I let neglect take its course, and the gun soon protested by spitting instead of spraying. A spray gun requires tender, loving care to function properly.

It doesn't take long, and it's certainly faster than trying to remove a built-up finish that's turned into an epoxy-like glaze.

Cleaning and lubrication techniques for spray guns commonly found in small shops, whether HVLP or turbine powered, are fairly similar.

Cleaning tools that come into contact with a spray gun should be firm enough to remove gummy finishes but not so hard that they damage the gun. The majority of gun manufacturers sell cleaning kits that include a skinny brush that fits inside difficult-to-reach places.

An old toothbrush also works well. I also keep a supply of round wooden toothpicks on hand for picking finish specks out of hard-to-reach places, such as deep inside the horns of an air cap.

After washing the cup, thoroughly clean the gasket that connects the cup to the gun. The cup is fixed with a gravity-fed gun; just remember to clean the cap and make sure the vent hole is clear. Unscrew the air cap and inspect for a dried or gummy finish.
A wooden toothpick will come in handy here. The use of wire or metal materials may cause the gun to malfunction.

Water-based finishes can dissolve dried lacquer or lacquer thinner, and lacquer can dissolve water-based finish that has been left in the gun.

The result is usually not pretty: As you make your final pass with the spray gun, a glob of gunk splatters on the tabletop. When transitioning from solvent-based finishes to water-based products, clean the gun with lacquer thinner first. The system should then be flushed with denatured alcohol, followed by water. Reverse the procedure when switching back.

Cleaning a gun removes some of the oil from critical joints, so replace the lubricant regularly. The lubricant should be designed for spray tools and should not contain silicone. Silicone ruins finish finishing depressions.

Once the silicone has entered your gun, it is difficult to remove, so be cautious about the lubricants you use in and around your tools.

Petroleum jelly will suffice if you don't have spray-gun lubricant. Avoid getting lubricant on the forward end of the fluid needle.

SPRAY GUN FOR CLEANING AND LUBING

Any moving or threaded part of a spray gun should be cleaned and lubricated. Use lubricant sparingly and avoid gelling any on the forward part of the fluid needle that contacts the finish. Never use silicone-containing lubricants.

Wash the Gasket

The gasket must be clean; otherwise, the gun will not seal properly and leak when tipped.

Cleare the Airways

The precisely machined air-cap orifices, which can become clogged with the finish, will not be harmed by wood toothpicks.

Remove the Air Cap and the Fluid Nozzle.

A skinny brush soaked in lacquer thinner is ideal for cleaning the inside of the gun.

Spraying a finish in a basement or garage was a risky business 25 years ago. You had no choice but to use high-pressure sprayers and flammable finishing materials, and spraying them without proper ventilation was a recipe for disaster.

Not only was there a high risk of a fire or explosion, but overspray was bound to settle on every horizontal surface in the immediate vicinity.

Spraying finishes at home or in a small shop has become a viable option thanks to new HVLP spray tools that drastically reduce overspray and new water-based finishes.

One problem remains: how to ventilate the overspray. While water-based finishes pose fewer fire hazards, the build-up of atomized finish and solvent can still pose a health risk.

Spraying in an enclosed space without adequate ventilation is prohibited, leaving you with only a few options:

- You can spray it outside. The disadvantage of this option is that dust, bugs, and other airborne debris frequently ruin your wet finish.
- Strong winds may also prevent the atomized spray from landing where you want it.
- Spray in a well-ventilated area, such as a screened-in porch. This is preferable because you reduce the possibility of debris landing on your wet finish and the force of sudden breezes, but you still have overspray to contend with.
- Spray in a confined space, such as a basement or garage, and exhaust the fumes with a fan. Nonetheless, basement windows are typically too small to accommodate a fan capable of moving enough air, and many garages lack windows entirely. These problems are solved by a small, portable spray booth.

Professional refinishers use specially designed spray booths to exhaust fumes in their shops, but these are quite expensive, with prices starting around $8,500 and rising depending on the number of bells and whistles.

These booths can also occupy a lot of floor space. The knockdown model can be built for a lot less money.

When not in use, it can be easily set up in a garage or basement with a large window and stored out of the way. The center of the explosion-proof motor drives a non-sparkling aluminum fan in the ventilation system. Even with non-flammable water-based finishes, I recommend at least a 16-inch fan and an explosion-proof motor.

Although the fumes are not flammable, the fine dust that accumulates around the intake and discharge openings is a potential source of ignition. Check your local electrical codes for the proper electrical connections for the fan. I installed the fan in a torsion-box style, which is both lightweight and strong.

To catch the overspray, I placed furnace filters in a slotted frame over the intake side of the fan. I added two lightweight wings to the main center panel, which are attached with removable loose-pin hinges and direct the airflow toward the fan.

They also make the assembly more portable and stable. A piece of cardboard or rigid insulation placed on top significantly improves airflow efficiency.

A hinged bracket on the outside of the middle panel prevents the assembly from tipping over while being assembled or disassembled.

I also added a foil-faced foam shroud to better direct the exhaust. The booth should be positioned so that the back of the fan exhausts through a large opening, such as an open window in a basement or a garage door opening.

To function properly, the amount of air consumed by the fan through exhaust must be replenished. This makeup air is critical, and it can enter the room through another open window or door.

I spray while rotating a workpiece on a simple 12-inch turntable. The turntable is made of steel bearings and is held together by two scraps of plywood.

I can work faster and more neatly if I can spin a workpiece while spraying. I can also mount the turntable on a stand for heavier objects.

Cart with wheels for easily transporting freshly sprayed pieces out of the booth.

To hang my spray guns, I screwed vinyl-coated hooks into the sides of the panels. Vinyl is non-sparking and holds metal parts more securely.
Guns have a nasty habit of falling over if not hung up due to the weight of the hose.

A turntable allows you to spray while rotating a workpiece, making the job go faster and the results look neater. This method is especially useful for spraying pieces with multiple sides or odd shapes.

A large, vinyl-coated hook for hanging the spray gun provides a safer, no-sparks alternative to metal-to-metal contact, and bright colors make the spray gun stand out. It is simple to find.

Chapter Nineteen

Spraying Setup

Few woodworkers can afford a custom-built spray booth, let alone one that complies with health and safety regulations for spraying solvent finishes. Waiting for a nice day and spraying outside, on the other hand, is fraught with complications.

The spray is blown back in your face by the wind, and every bug in the neighborhood dive-bombs the wet finish. The spray booth and accessories will allow you to spray indoors in a controlled environment for less than $400.

The booth is only for water-based finishes. I recommend that you do not spray flammable materials indoors unless you remove the top cut-out for the furnace box fan filter to support the fan and you have a ventilation system. A dedicated room outfitted with an explosion-proof fan and lighting fixtures

When spraying indoors, it's critical to remove the gun's overspray, not only for health reasons but also to keep the atomized overspray from settling on your furniture and creating a rough surface.

A simple solution is to build a booth out of three panels of foil-faced rigid foam insulation joined together with duct tape. Glued furring strips to a fourth top panel that keeps the booth stable

Make a 30-inch-off-the-floor hole in the center panel. Place a furnace filter in front of the hole and a box fan on the sawhorses outside. Use a low-cost open weave filter; more expensive filters designed to trap minute particles will become clogged with finish far too quickly.

The 4-foot-by-8-foot foam panels are easily cut to fit any location, and when folded for storage, the booth is less than 2 feet deep and light enough to be carried by one person.

Unless you don't mind spraying the floor, lay down a cotton drop cloth. Plastic sheeting should not be used because it becomes slippery when wet.

Save large sheets of cardboard packaging for test spraying when adjusting the fan pattern or setting up the gun.

Drive several nails or drywall screws through a piece of cheap plywood. This nail board assists during and after spraying. Finish the piece's no-show side first, then place it on the points while you finish the show side.

Because the workpiece must be allowed to dry on the board, you will need a separate board for each part you spray during each session. A finishing turntable enables you to turn the workpiece rather than walking around it and enduring spraying toward the fan.

A simple finishing turntable can be made by resting a nail board on top of a 12-in. dia. plate on a plywood base. Place the finishing turntable on sawhorses to raise the workpiece to a comfortable height and even with the fan for better fume extraction.

Place the finishing turntable on the floor or rest the work on a dolly for larger pieces. Spray-gun holders give the gun a place to rest. Most cup and pressure feed guns have an integrated hook that can be hung from plastic-coated hooks.

Gravity-style guns necessitate the use of a gravity-gun filling station, which also serves as convenient strainer support. Using building adhesive, adhere a piece of 8-inch-thick plywood to the foam spray booth, then screw on the gun holder.

Always strain the finish through a cone to remove impurities filter through the gun Most water-based clear finishes benefit from a medium-mesh filter.

To keep contamination from the compressor from reaching the gun, purchase some inline air filters from an auto supply store. When spraying, you will need bright lighting in the booth to distinguish between wet and dry areas. On a tripod, I like to use halogen work lights.

Chapter Twenty

Spraying Setup

Unfortunately, so few woodworkers have begun spray finishing. The main reason is a lack of information, and manufacturers bear a large portion of the blame.

Professional spray systems assume you're already familiar with spraying, while entry-level tool manuals provide only basic information and instructions on cans of finish direct you to your spray-gun manual.

To address this information gap, I'll describe the various types of spray guns and explain how to match the gun to the finish.

By spraying various pieces of furniture, I can determine which spray strokes work best on each type of surface. This information will enable you to start finishing like the pros, so let's get started.

Atomization is the process by which a spray gun combines pressurized air and liquid finish. It is critical to adjust the gun to the thickness, or viscosity, of the finish you want to spray for proper atomization.

A viscosity measuring cup is a small container with a precisely machined hole at the bottom. Most turbine-driven spray guns come with this type of cup, but conversion gun owners can buy one for around $35. Because viscosity is affected by temperature, make sure the finish is at 70°F before attempting to measure it. Begin by immersing the cup in the finish and then removing it.

Begin timing when the top rim of the cup breaks the finish's surface. Raise the clip 6 in. over the can and stop the clock when the first break appears in the fluid stream. The number of seconds elapsed is a measure of the viscosity of the finish.

Once you've determined the viscosity of the finish, you can choose the appropriate needle/nozzle and, in some cases, the air cap. Keep in mind that different types of guns (gravity, suction, or pressure feed) use different needle/nozzle sizes to achieve the same finish. Always use the smallest needle or nozzle possible, as smaller-diameter ones atomize finish the best. Before using a larger needle or nozzle, try thinning the product first.

Some low-cost guns may only come with one size needle or nozzle, and in some cases, the manual may not even specify which size needle or nozzle is included.

In this case, thin the finish until good atomization is achieved. Water-based finish manufacturers typically recommend thinning with no more than 5% to 10% distilled water.

Beyond that, you'll need to use a viscosity decrease designed specifically for that finish. Add the water or reducer in 1 oz. increments per quart of finish until it sprays properly.

It is best to strain all finishes as you pour them into the gun for the best finish. To strain impurities from water-based clear finishes, use a fine or medium mesh cone filter; for paint, use a medium-mesh filter.

Make final adjustments to the gun after you've matched the finish. Also, choose a respirator with cartridges that are appropriate for the type of finish you will be spraying.

HVLP spray guns have a maximum inlet pressure ranging from 20 psi to 50 psi; the precise figure is either stamped on the gun's body or specified in the instructions.

Conversion or compressor-driven, HVLP spray guns are designed to reduce this inlet pressure to 10 psi at the nozzle, which is sufficient to atomize most finishes.

Set the compressor's regulator to some extent above with the trigger of the gun partially depressed to release air but not completely this is the maximum inlet pressure

This allows for hose pressure drop caused by friction as air flows through the hose. Install a mini regulator at the gun to set the pressure to avoid this calculation.

Close the fan-width and fluid-delivery valves by turning them clockwise. Check to see if your gun has a cheater valve. While the trigger is fully depressed, turn the fluid delivery valve a few turns to control the amount of fluid that flows through the nozzle.

Set it to a low setting for delicate spraying of edges and small areas, or a high setting for spraying large surfaces. Spray some scrap wood or corrugated cardboard.

A fine and uniform pattern of droplets across the width of the spray is ideal. If the droplets are coarse and large, either the finish is too thin or the needle or nozzle is too large.

If the gun sputters or spits, the opposite is true. If the finish looks good, reduce the air pressure in 8-psi increments until the finish forms a dimpled surface resembling an orange peel.

If the dried finish does not budge when prodded with a toothpick, dissolve it with a soft brush and lacquer thinner. A dirty air cap is frequently to blame for poor spray pattern or atomization.

If your gun hasn't been thoroughly cleaned in a while, you may need to disassemble it to access gummed-up parts. To clean the inside of the gun, use a long, skinny brush dipped in lacquer thinner.

Smaller parts can be soaked in lacquer thinner, but any rubber O-rings should be avoided because the lacquer thinner will cause them to swell.

While the O-rings will eventually shrink back to normal, reassembling the gun while the rubber is swollen can damage them. Replace any torn or worn-out O-rings.

You must take extra precautions if you spray both water and solvent-based finishes with the same gun.

Then increase the air pressure by 5 psi. Take note of this as the correct air pressure for the finish you're using. By reducing bounce-back and overspray, operating the gun at the lowest pressure possible saves material. The spray pattern is controlled by the gun's fan-width control valve. The spray pattern expands as the valve is opened.

When you open the valve, you may have to increase the air pressure going into the gun; therefore, keep an eye on your regulator. Open the cheater valve on the gun completely. The correct air or liquid balance is determined in the same manner as with a conversion gun.

Nonetheless, the shape and orientation of the spray pattern on most turbine guns are determined by the position of the air cap.

When the air cap's horns are horizontal, the spray pattern is broad and vertically oriented.

The spray pattern is horizontal when the air cap is rotated 90 degrees. The spray pattern is tight and round due to the intermediate position. Before spraying any furniture, disassemble large items as much as possible.

If possible, remove backs from carcass pieces and drawer bottoms. Consider finishing slats before final assembly if you have a complex project that includes a lot of them.

Because of the ease of laying down a finish, inexperienced sprayers frequently apply too much at once. Each coat should be about two-thousandths of an inch thick, or two mils in spraying terms.

A mil gauge is a piece of metal with teeth that are spaced in mil increments. Spray some finish onto an impermeable surface, such as laminate or glass, to use the gauge. Press down as you drag the gauge through the wet finish, keeping it 90 degrees to the surface. Withdraw the gauge and make a note of the first tooth that isn't finished, as well as the one next to it that is.

Your depth of finish will be a thickness in the middle of these two marks. If you're having trouble seeing clear finishes on the gauge, sprinkling talc on wet teeth and blowing it off will help. Talc will adhere to wet teeth.

To practice, place a flat board or a piece of cardboard on a pair of sawhorses. Hold the gun perpendicular to the surface, 6 to 8 inches away, and 3 inches from the bottom left-hand corner. Depress the trigger until the finish appears, then move the gun across the board until it is 2 to 3 inches past the far edge.

Instead of arcing your pass, lock your forearm so that the gun moves across the board in a straight line and at a constant height.

Make a second pass that overlaps the first by 50 to 75 percent. Move the gun quickly enough to avoid puddles of finish, but not so quickly that the surface feels rough after drying.

To reduce overspray landing on the wet finish and leaving it rough, I start with the surface closest to me and work my way toward the exhaust fan in my spray booth.

Because this basic stroke is essential to all spraying, practice it until it becomes second nature.

A crosshatch is the most basic spray technique for flat surfaces begin with the piece's underside: Begin your first pass at a 90-degree angle to the grain and spray a series of overlapping strokes on the edge closest to you.

Then, using a turntable, rotate the top 90 degrees and spray with the grain. Turn the panel over and reposition it on the nail board while holding the still-dry edges.

Spray the edges parallel to the surface, then bring the gun up to 45 degrees to the top and spray them again for an extra finish.

Finally, cross-hatch the top side once more. If a drip occurs and you won't be damaging a delicate toner or glaze underneath, wipe it away with your finger and re-spray the area.

Spraying inside a cabinet becomes much easier when the back is removed. If you can't get rid of the back, you'll get a face full of overspray unless you reduce the air pressure drastically, which may result in a poorly atomized finish.

Begin with the underside of the top, followed by the two sides, leaving the bottom last so that overspray does not settle and create a rough finish.
Spray all four edges of each panel before moving on to the center.
Rotate the piece so that the spray is always directed toward the back of the surface.

Apply overlapping strokes from bottom to top, but do not spray across the grain, as too much finish will sag or run on a vertical surface.

The fan will then draw the overspray away from the piece. Blow away the finished cloud left inside by depressing the trigger of the gun to the point where air but no finish comes through.

Begin at the bottom and work your way up, applying a continuous layer of finish until you reach the top.

Overlap each pass 50% as if spraying a flat surface, but don't crosshatch, as the extra finish will cause runs.

If possible, adjust the fan width to match the width of the frame members for face frames.

Work from the least visible parts of a stool or chair to the most visible. Spray the underside and inside areas of the piece while it is upside down. They must still be completed, despite being less visible.

To prevent the finish from pooling around the bottom of the legs, flip the stool over and rest it on four screws driven into the feet. Spray the sides of the legs and the slats next, working quickly to apply light coats.

Finally, finish the most visible outside surfaces. The trick, as with vertical surfaces, is to keep the coats of finish thin and avoid sags and runs.

STEPS:
STEP 1 – BEGIN WITH THE END IN MIND MEASURE THE VISCOSITY IN **STEP 2**
Immerse the viscosity cup in the finish and time how long it takes for the finishing stream to break.

STEP 3 – CHOOSE THE APPROPRIATE NEEDLE OR NOZZLE
The larger the needle or nozzle to achieve good atomization, the higher the viscosity of the finish.

STEP 4 – FINISH FILTERS
To catch impurities that could clog the spray gun, strain the finish through a cone filter.

ADJUST THE GUN IN **STEP 5**

STEP 6 - CONFIGURE THE AIR PRESSURE

Set the gun's trigger to allow only air to pass through while the trigger is depressed outlet air pressure at the compressor, adjusted for hose pressure drop.

DIAL THE SPRAY PATTERNS IN **STEP 7**

The technique for adjusting the shape and orientation of the spray pattern will be determined by the type of gun.

STEP 8 – TWO ADJUSTMENTS ARE REQUIRED FOR CONVERSION GUNS

The pattern is changed from circular to elongate by a valve in the back. The spray pattern's orientation can be changed by twisting the air cap.

Rather than changing your grip on the gun, change the spray pattern to suit the object being sprayed.

A horizontal pattern provides the best coverage for vertical surfaces; when spraying flat panels in the crosshatch pattern, adjust the gun to get a vertical pattern. When finishing narrow parts like slats and legs, a tight circular pattern reduces overspray.

STEP 9 – THE FRONT TURBINE GUNS ARE ADJUSTED

Simply turn the air cap to change the pattern from circular to horizontal to vertical.

THE ESSENTIAL SPRAY STROKE

For the entire pass over the surface, keep the spray gun at the same distance from the workpiece. Begin spraying from the edge of the workpiece and work your way across the surface. Stop spraying from the other side.

IN FOUR STEPS, COMPLETE A PANEL

A good finish on a flat panel requires even coverage on all surfaces. Using a nail board and turntable, you can finish the top surface while the bottom is still wet and direct the spray and overspray toward an extractor fan.

APPLY TO THE EDGES

Make one pass on all four edges with the gun parallel to the panel's surface.

RESTORE THE EDGES

Apply a second coat of finish to the edges with the gun at a 450 angle to the panel.

WORKING WITH RUNS

If you find an area with too much finish, quickly wipe it away and apply another light coat.

APPLY TO THE GRAIN

Spray overlapping strokes across the grain while keeping the gun at an even height over the surface.

THEN APPLY THE GRAIN SPRAY

Turn the workpiece 90 degrees and spray the second half of a crosshatch pattern with the grain.

Chapter Twenty One

How to Spray Furniture

First, spray the undersides of the shelves. Then, finish the inside of a cabinet by spraying the sides, followed by the shelf tops. As a result, the most visible surface is sprayed last and is not affected by overspray.

Apply overlapping strokes from bottom to top, but do not spray across the grain, as too much finish will sag or run on a vertical surface.

Spray the undersides of the rails and the least visible interior surfaces. Spray the visible areas while keeping the spray gun at the same distance from the work piece. Do the same for the tabletop, but add the first pass with the gun angled around the inside edge of the frame. Apply a crosshatch spray pattern to glass-panel doors as a flat, continuous surface.

Many woodworkers I know are uninterested in, if not afraid of, spray finishing. They believe the tools are too mysterious, expensive, and difficult to master.

The inverse is true. There are numerous low-cost, easy-to-use spray systems available. It took me less time to master a spray gun than it did to master a router.

Best of all, the finish on a gun is often so smooth that I don't need to rub it out.

Following sound spraying principles and knowing how to use the tools allows me to create virtually flaw-free finishes.

Spraying is best done in a booth, where a powerful exhaust removes overspray and dust from the air. When spraying solvent-borne finishes, you don't have a choice but to use an explosion-proof spray booth.

However, they are expensive. Waterborne finishes don't require explosion-proof tools, and they're getting better all the time. You only need a well-ventilated and clean location.

If you have enough floor space, you can construct a spray room with an exhaust fan and intake filters to ensure a consistent supply of clean, fresh air. Check with your local building officials first, no matter where you intend to spray.

It is just as important to prepare the surface as it is to spray the finish. For stained work, I typically raise the grain with a damp cloth, let the surface dry, and sand with 220 grit before spraying.

I sand to 180 grit and spray a light coat of dye stain or finish before applying waterborne finishes and dyes. This raises the grain and stiffens the fibers, making 220-grit sanding easier.

Spray paint or pigmented lacquers require more effort. Opaque finishes draw attention to minor flaws. Before the wood can be sprayed, it usually needs at least two rounds of filling, sanding, and priming.

It would be simpler if you could just pour the finish straight from the can into a spray bottle and start applying it. However, you may need to thin it on occasion.
Which thinner you use and how much you add will be determined by the material you're applying, the spray system you're using, and the purpose of the piece.

Some manufacturers provide inadequate thinning information. Use the appropriate thinner if it is listed on the label. Some cans of finish do not list a thinner because the contents do not need to be thinned.

If this is the case, you can usually thin the finish with the recommended clean-up solvent. A finish's viscosity is a measure of its resistance to flow.

Thinning a finish reduces its viscosity, allowing the spray gun to break it down into smaller particles more easily. The smoother the appearance, the finer the atomization.

Thinners can eliminate common spray issues such as orange peel, but when used incorrectly, thinners can cause problems. Waterborne finishes are particularly susceptible to thinning.

Overthinking the finish can prevent it from forming a clear, hard film. Some spray-gun manufacturers recommend a specific needle or tip combination's finish viscosity.

This data can be presented as a ratio or as a percentage of thinner and finish. The viscosity can also be expressed as the number of seconds required to empty a specific size viscosity cup.

Small holes in the bottom of viscosity cups allow liquid to drain through. Most spray system manufacturers sell appropriately sized cups.

Temperature and humidity have a big impact on how much thinner to use in a finish and how well it sprays. Spraying is difficult in conditions of low temperature and high humidity.

Even if you strictly adhere to all of the labels, you may need to adjust the amount of thinner you use. You can keep track of how much thinner you require for various conditions. You'll get the hang of it after a while.

Because a speck of dirt or dried finish can ruin the job, your finish and tools should be as clean as possible.

Pour the finish through a strainer or filter available at paint supply stores to remove impurities.

You can take extra precautions by installing a filter on the end of the dip tube that draws the finish from the pot, or by installing an in-line filter near the gun.

To keep the air coming from the compressor dry and clean, I run it through a canister-type separator, which filters out water, oil, and other contaminants and dirt before they enter the hose that supplies air to the gun

The amount of finish that is deposited on a surface is controlled by the fluid tip in a spray gun. Lighter finishes, in general, necessitate a small tip. Larger fluid tips are required for denser materials or those with a higher percentage of solids.

The spray gun's air cap regulates the velocity of the air, which determines how finely the fluid is atomized. Air caps with smaller holes cause the air to leave the gun at a faster rate, resulting in finer atomization.

To achieve peak performance, air caps are combined with fluid tips. Most guns come with a standard setup that is suitable for a variety of finishes. The system includes a 0.5-inch-diameter fluid tip and a corresponding air cap.

The standard setup will produce acceptable results with most finishes, but it's worth experimenting with different fluid tip and air cap combinations from time to time.

Because the amount of air feeding the gun in a turbine-driven HVLP system is continuous, air pressure adjustments can only be made by changing air caps.

When using a waterborne finish with a turbine and a bleeder-type gun, keep the nozzle clean. Blobs of finish drying on the air cap and blemishing the work are common with these guns.

Spray guns have air and fluid adjustments. The type of finish being sprayed, the size of the object to be coated, and the speed of application all influence how the fluid and air are controlled.

I always test my fan pattern and finish delivery rate on scrap wood or cardboard before spraying the piece to make adjustments. It is simple to adjust a turbine-powered spray gun: The goal, regardless of the type of gun you own, is to get the air flowing through the gun first, then gradually introduces the finish until it flows continuously and evenly

The gun should spray a complete, wet coat with no heavy spots or missed spots. From here, you can adjust the spray rate and fan pattern by turning either knob.

If you need to spray a large amount of material quickly, increase the fluid control setting. When coating large surfaces, expand the fan pattern.

If you want to achieve a fine finish or spray small items, restricting the fan and fluid will give you more control over how much finish is applied and where it lands.

But keep in mind that how you turn one knob affects the other. For example, increasing the airflow and out-adjusting the fluid may result in an overly fine finish.

Opening the fluid control without widening the fan, on the other hand, can result in runs and sags. The finish will coat evenly and flow together well at the optimal settings.

You can control the air pressure entering the gun as well as the fluid rate and fan shape with high-pressure spray guns and conversion-air HVLP guns, both of which are powered by a compressor.

Getting all three adjustments to work together can be difficult and requires some trial and error, but being able to control the air pressure at the gun gives you more spraying options.

Whatever the size and shape of the object you're spraying, the main thing to remember is to apply an even coat to the entire piece.

Spray the finish in several thin coats rather than one thick coat. Lighter coats are less likely to run, dry faster, and allow for easier sanding between coats.

If the pieces you're spraying are so small that the gun's air blows them everywhere, try placing them on a piece of screen or wire mesh. Because the spray is softer, I prefer spraying small parts with my turbine HVLP gun. Spraying several small pieces at once is a good production tip for spraying numerous small pieces.

Rotate the turntable as you spray to avoid applying too thick a coat to the pieces. Place large pieces of furniture on sawhorses or a stand at a comfortable height.

While spraying, you should not have to bend, reach, or otherwise contort your arm or body. You should be able to easily turn and move the work.

I occasionally assist with the work on stickers or points to ensure that the bottom edge is adequately covered. There are a few things to keep in mind to ensure even spray coverage. Firmly grip the gun, but not so tightly that your hand becomes tired or uncomfortable.

Point the gun's nose perpendicular to the work surface, and keep the gun the same distance away from the work on each pass.

Move the gun in a straight line, not an arcing, sweeping motion. Begin your stroke about 6 inches before the gun is over the wood, and continue for the same distance on the other side.

Trigger the gun a split second after you begin your motion, and keep spraying until your arm comes to a complete stop. Move your arm steadily and smoothly across the piece, without changing speed.

Hold the gun 6 to 8 inches from the surface for most HVLP guns. This allows you to spray a full, wet coat with little overspray and good coverage. Move the gun at the same rate as you would a brush.

Each pass should roughly overlap the previous one by half. Reduce the flow and move the gun closer when spraying small objects or in tight spaces. Work from the inside corners out to avoid overspray clouds and bounce-back. Increase your wrist action and trigger faster. Increase the flow, pull the gun back an inch or two, and make passes over large areas in the opposite direction

To make a tack coat, I lightly spray across the grain. Then I spray with grain right away. When your spray passes intersect, such as the stretcher-to-leg joint of a chair, release the trigger a little sooner than usual.

This will soften the finish. Mask off adjacent areas if overlapping passes continue to be an issue. It's easy to forget that after spraying a piece, the finish requires a warm, dry, and dust-free environment to cure. If you don't have a separate drying area, your shop's production can come to a halt.

Even with a designated area, storing a large number of wet cabinets, doors, drawers, and trim pieces can be difficult. I use a rack system to dry components and store them for short periods.

When I bake, I use plywood trays slipped into old baker's racks.

Many small pieces must be dried. When I'm drying round or unusual items, such as balusters, I hang them from an overhead wire using swivel hooks

Each piece is rotated and sprayed before being hung in my drying area. While my work is drying, I make it a point to thoroughly clean my spray gun.

I dry the parts with compressed air after cleaning them with the solvent recommended for the finish. After that, I coat all of the fluid passages with alcohol and allow it to evaporate before storing the gun in its case.

Perform a dry run of the entire procedure before spraying. To avoid overcoating or missing areas, visualize and then practice the spray stroke sequence.

While the order in which you spray parts of a piece may vary, there are a few general guidelines to follow:

Begin with the least visible areas, such as drawer bottoms and cabinet backs, and work your way up to the visible parts.

Spray the edges of tabletops, doors, and shelves before the tops, for example. This reduces overspray on the most visible surfaces. Working from the inside out applies to case pieces.

Working from the wettest edge allows you to easily blend areas you've just sprayed. Move the gun away from your body and toward the exhaust fan whenever possible.

This will keep overspray from settling on previously sprayed areas and will also provide you with a clear view.

1. Spray the overhead corners first, then fill in the inside top.
2. Coat the back and sides of the interior. These areas will not be visible once the piece is completed.
3. Shelf tops and fronts always overlap strokes.
4. Complete the face frame. Start with the inside edges and work your way to the front of the case.
5. Exterior cabinet slides and front corners
6. Apply on top. the most visible part of the case is not marred by overspray by leaving the top for last.

Chapter Twenty Two

Finishes

It's a rare woodworker who isn't intimidated by the solvent cans that line the shelves of a hardware store. The multisyllabic names evoke memories of less-than-productive high school chemistry classes, and the dire health warnings are equally unsettling.

The temptation is to grab something vaguely familiar, hope it's compatible with the finish you're using and dash out the door. But it doesn't have to be this way.

I'll walk you through the world of solvents, explaining the good, bad, and unpronounceable. I'll explain which solvents are appropriate for spraying, brushing, or wiping on water or oil-based finishes, shellacs, or solvent lacquers. Let's get started.

Almost all finishing materials contain volatile liquids, which evaporate during the drying and curing processes. These liquids, known as solvents and thinners, make the finishing material less viscous, making it easier to apply.

Solvents and thinners are distinguished by chemists: Solvents dissolve or break up finishing resins and reduce viscosity, whereas thinners only reduce viscosity.

The only time a woodworker will use a solvent is to dissolve shellac flakes in denatured alcohol. As many woodworkers do, I use the terms solvent and thinner interchangeably in this chapter.

I've classified finishes into four groups based on the toxicity of their solvents: water-based, shellac-based, oil-based, and solvent-based lacquer. For each family, I discuss the available compatible thinners and the factors to consider when selecting one.

Water-based finishes are relatively new, and the chemistry behind them is still being refined in some cases. Water-based lacquer and polyurethane are well-known among woodworkers, but water-based varnish, a gel stain, and Danish oil finishes are also available.

While the novice may believe that because they are mostly water, they would be the easiest to thin, their chemical complexity makes them the least forgiving finishes to tamper with. If you add too much water, you can cause serious problems.

More than 5% to 10% is usually fine for viscosity adjustments to make it spray or brush better, but more than that can disrupt the chemical makeup of the finish, affecting how the finish forms a film.

A retarder is a better option for a finish that dries too quickly. In hot, dry weather, a retarder is typically used.

It aids in the prevention of orange peel by allowing the finish more time to flow out and achieve a level surface. Use a retarder that has been recommended by the finish manufacturer.

The wrong retarder can throw the finish's chemical balance off. When spraying a water-based finish, try to compensate for viscosity by using a larger needle or nozzle and adjusting your finishing environment or technique before adding water or a retarder.

Spray thinner coats when the weather is hot and humid, and set up fans to gently blow air across the finish as it dries.

Shellac is one of the oldest woodworking finishes. No other finish can match the depth and clarity it adds to wood, but its lack of resilience makes it unsuitable for heavily used surfaces.

Shellac is available as dried flakes that must be dissolved in alcohol or as a ready-to-use liquid. Denatured alcohol is the best all-around thinner for both preblended shellac and shellac flakes.

The solvents evaporate as the shellac is sprayed, cooling the workpiece's surface.

When the temperature falls below the dew point, moisture condenses on the surface, resulting in a cloudy finish known as blushing. To avoid blushing when spraying shellac in hot, humid weather, slow down the drying rate.

Butanol or isopropanol are suitable retarders, with the latter being available at auto parts stores as gas-line antifreeze.

Do not use rubbing alcohol; while the active ingredient is isopropanol, the remaining 30 to 50% is water, which will not advance your finish.

Glycol ether, which is used as a lacquer retarder, also slows the drying time of shellac, but the finish may become soft and easily damaged.

When brushing shellac on a large surface, such as a tabletop, a retarder is also useful. If the shellac dries too quickly, you risk applying the finish to an area where the finish has already begun to set up, preventing the brush stroke edges from blending.

A teaspoon of pure gum spirit turpentine in 4 oz. of liquid shellac acts as a retarder.

With the addition of a retarder, the first line of finish will remain wet until the second line is brushed on and the two can be blended. Linseed, Tung, and Danish oils, oil-based varnishes and polyurethanes, oil paint, and waxes comprise the most extensive family of finishes and are the products that most woodworkers consider when it comes to finishing.

Thinners for these finishes come in two varieties: hydrocarbons and terpenes. Petroleum oil is a source of hydrocarbons such as kerosene, mineral spirits, naphtha, paint thinner, toluene, and xylene.

Terpenes (turpentine, d-limonene) are derived from plants, with turpentine originating in pine trees and d-limonene originating in citrus trees.

These two solvents can almost always be used in place of hydrocarbons. D-limonene has a distinct citrus aroma that makes it more pleasant to work with, but it is difficult to find.

It has similar toxicity and flammability to mineral spirits but evaporates at a slower rate. Because of the high cost of extracting turpentine, mineral spirits have largely replaced this traditional thinner.

One disadvantage of using turpentine is that the rosin content varies depending on which trees were processed in each batch. If the rosin content of the, can you're using is high, the finish will be soft; however, there is no measurement on the side of the can.

Mineral spirits and naphtha are the two best thinners to use. Mineral spirits are best for brushing and keeping a wet edge, whereas naphtha is better for spraying or wiping.
Kerosene can be added to oil-based stains in very small amounts (6 to 12 drops per pint) to slow them down for easier application on large surfaces.
Commercial furniture makers and professional finishers have traditionally relied on solvent-based lacquer finishes.

They are not as popular among hobbyists due to their reputation for requiring costly spraying facilities. Lacquer thinner, a mixture of ketones, alcohol, and hydrocarbons, is used to thin solvent-based lacquer.

Manufacturers can tailor a thinner to be fast, medium, or slow evaporating by adjusting the ratio of these components.

Most woodworking finish suppliers only keep medium-speed thinner on hand. An auto-finishing store is a great place to find fast and slow-evaporating lacquer thinners.

Fast-evaporating thinner prevents sagging on vertical surfaces, but acetone will suffice if you can't find it.

Unless you are spraying in extremely low humidity, an acetone-thinned finish is susceptible to blushing due to its rapid evaporation rate.

Slow-evaporating thinners make it easier for the finish to flow out and level on horizontal surfaces. As a result, the slow-evaporating thinner is sometimes referred to as "warm weather" thinner.

As an alternative to slow-evaporating thinner, mix lacquer retarder with standard lacquer thinner before applying it to a finish. One reason for using solvents is to control how quickly the finish dries. This level of control is desirable for any application technique.

When spraying a vertical surface, a slow drying time may cause the finish to run, whereas a fast-drying time may leave an orange-peel appearance. When brushing, the right solvent can keep the edge wet while not attracting dust by taking forever to dry. A solvent's drying time is the same as if it acts as a retarder, which means it slows down the drying time.

A medium rating indicates that the solvent has little effect on the drying properties of a finish, while any thinned finish will dry faster. And fast solvents do exactly that: they shorten the drying time. The actual speed will vary depending on the application techniques used and the environmental conditions.

Mineral spirits and naphtha were brushed onto a board at the same time. Three minutes later, the naphtha has almost completely evaporated, but the mineral spirits remain wet. Water-based finishes have the most difficult evaporation rate to adjust of all the finishing families.

They typically require a specific retarder, with plain water being used sparingly. Brushing should be applied without leaving lap marks. Add a small amount of retarder to a water-based finish if you have trouble keeping a wet edge because the finish dries too quickly, which can happen in hot, dry weather.

Chapter Twenty Three

Using the Proper Solvent Gloves

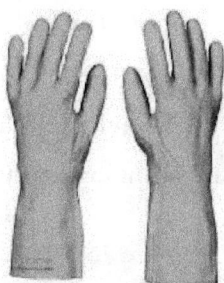

Most woodworkers use disposable latex or vinyl gloves when working with solvents.

Eventually, a specific solvent appears to eat through the glove as if it weren't there, resulting in chapped skin or even chemical burns. There are disposable and reusable latex, nitrile, vinyl, and neoprene gloves available.

Less important than the material of the glove is to remember that disposable gloves should only be used for splash protection, such as when blending or brushing on a finish.

Use heavy-duty gloves for prolonged contacts, such as when cleaning a spray gun with a solvent or wiping on a finish.

Unfortunately, no single glove is appropriate for all solvents. Specific information on how different glove materials react to various solvents can be found on the websites of each manufacturer.

Latex

Latex is primarily used for combining dye powders and applying water-based dyes.

The main benefit of disposable latex gloves is their flexibility and feel, which makes them ideal for detailed work. Neither of the gloves shown is resistant to oils or hydrocarbon derivatives (mineral spirits, naphtha, paint thinner, or kerosene).

Nitrile

Nitrile gloves protect against almost any solvent that a woodworker is likely to use. The only exception is a solvent containing a ketone, such as acetone.

The disposable version provides more protection than the other two types of disposable gloves, but they are more difficult to find and more expensive.

Vinyl

Vinyl is suitable for powdered dyes as well as dyes in water solutions. Disposable vinyl gloves are the least expensive option, but they tear more easily than disposable latex gloves. Keep away from ketones and aromatic solvents. Denser gloves provide better protection but have a clumsier feel.

Neoprene

Except for lacquer thinner, where nitrile is preferable, neoprene gloves are an excellent choice for regular contact with most solvents.

Chapter Twenty Four

Aerosol Finishes

When the actuator is pushed down, a small valve opens, allowing the can's head pressure to force a mixture of finish resin, solvent, and propellant up the dip tube and out the nozzle.

A liquefied propellant instantly vaporizes as the finish solution leaves the tip, exploding the finish and solvent mixture into millions of droplets.

Because the dip tube and actuator orifice of a typical aerosol can are so small in comparison to the corresponding parts of a spray gun, the liquid finish in the can must be very thin to spray properly.

As a result, most aerosol finishes contain less than half the solids and significantly more solvents than their non-aerosol counterparts in the same volume.

A high solvent-to-solids ratio is a recipe for runs, drips, and sags. These difficulties are simply avoided.

When it comes to nozzle design, not all aerosol cans are created equal. Some aerosols spray an evenly formed tapered fan pattern, similar to the best conventional spray guns, whereas basic aerosol nozzles produce a simple doughnut-shaped cone pattern.

Aerosol nozzles that fan out the finish are easier to control and provide fewer runs in my experience than those that spray conical patterns.

Remove the cap and inspect the nozzle when shopping for an aerosol finish. Fan nozzles will be made of two plastic pieces: a large button actuator and a small plastic disc inserted in the face. A raised line runs across the orifice of this easily identified disc.

The disc can be rotated to create a vertical or horizontal fan, which is useful when spraying large areas.

Cone spray actuators, on the other hand, are made of one or two pieces of plastic and do not have a line.

Pick up a plastic trigger handle while you're there. This handle improves control and reduces finger fatigue, transforming a simple spray can into a functional spray gun.

Finishing requires a high level of cleanliness, especially when using aerosol cans. When it comes to dirt or grime, heavy-bodied brush-on finishes are more forgiving: they tend to bridge over the offending contamination, whereas thin aerosol finishes frequently pull away from it.

Dust produces an uneven stippled appearance in the dry finish, whereas oily or waxy residue produces a moon-cratered appearance on the dried surface.

Before you begin, make sure that all surfaces to be finished are free of dirt and grease, because fixing the problem after the fact requires sanding off the entire finish and starting over.

Before beginning the finishing ritual, I make it a habit to thoroughly vacuum the sanding dust from my ventures, as opposed to wiping with a tack rag, which simply moves the dust around.

Chapter Twenty Five

Accurate Technique Yields

Spraying with an aerosol can is a simple technique that can be learned quickly, but as with any new finishing technique or product, practice on scrap until you are comfortable.

Shake the can vigorously up and down for a minute, or until any agitator balls inside are loose, then swirl for one minute to combine the ingredients.

To ensure that the ingredients stay well blended, swirl the can infrequently during the finishing job.

I get better results if I start spraying from the front of the venture and work my way back, but feel free to experiment.

The distance between the can and the surface is determined by the spray nozzle geometry, the amount and type of propellant in the can, and the viscosity of the liquid, but in general, the distance ranges from 6 in. to 12 in. Follow the manufacturer's instructions on the can's side.

Trigger the aerosol can 2 in. to 3 in. off the edge of the piece and move it across the entire width in one smooth motion, finally releasing the trigger 2 in. to 3 in. past the other edge.

This method eliminates puddling at the start and end of the stroke. Short bursts of spray, stopping at the end of each stroke Repeat the procedure, overlapping each successive swath by approximately 50% until the entire surface is covered.

Turn the piece 90 degrees and apply another light coat, referred to as boxing in spray finishing jargon. Avoid wearing heavy coats. It is much easier to spray another coat than to sand out a run.

Allow the finish to dry before repeating the process until you are satisfied with the result. The number of coats required for maximum protection varies according to the percentage of solids in the individual finish.

For decorative projects, I apply multiple coats until the pores of tight-grained wood are filled with the finish. After that, ventures that will see a lot of us get two or three more coats.

In general, I prefer satin finishes because they conceal flaws that a gloss finish would highlight. The method for rubbing Oil in an aerosol finish is the same as for any other type of finish.

Nonetheless, because each coat of finish is so thin, it is possible to sand out any flaws like dust specks, apply a final show coat, and buff with a dry rag to achieve a silky-smooth finish.

After use, always clear the nozzle by turning the can upside down and spraying on some scrap until nothing but propellant comes out of the nozzle. As a result, the actuator will not be clogged with a dried finish the next time you use it. When it's hot and humid, don't spray.

Most aerosol finishes work best at temperatures around 75°F and low relative humidity, which are rarely found in most woodshops.
The solvent in a conventional spray finish can be adjusted to suit different atmospheric conditions, but because aerosol finishes come in a sealed pressurized can, you cannot adjust the solvent mixture to account for less-than-ideal conditions.

This means that when sprayed on a hot, humid day, some finishes will almost certainly blush. Blush occurs when the rapid evaporation of a finish's solvent cools the surface to below the dew point of the hot, humid air surrounding it.

On the surface of this cool finish, water vapor in the air condenses into liquid water. This causes some of the finished resin to crystallize, resulting in microscopic white specks on f a solid finish.

Avoiding blush is simple: don't finish when the temperature and humidity are both high.

All is not lost if you end up with blush on your venture. It is usually removed by waiting for the humidity to decrease and then spritzing a light coat of the same finish over the entire project.

The solvents in the fresh coat frequently release the trapped moisture in the dried finish, resulting in the removal of the blush. You can also reduce the likelihood of blushing if you match your finish to the weather.

I've discovered through trial and error that aerosol acrylic lacquer finishes blush less than aerosol nitrocellulose lacquer finishes when it's hot and humid, whereas aerosol varnishes are virtually blush-proof all year.

Aerosol finishes, without a doubt, are a valuable asset in any shop due to their ready-to-use, spray-it-and-forget-it nature.

However, this convenience comes at a cost. The warnings on aerosol finish cans go something like this: Propane, isobutane, and petroleum distillates are included. Vapor \shameful. Not to be punctured or incinerated. Heat or prolonged exposure to the sun can cause bursting.

Take note of these critical warnings. That seemingly innocuous aerosol can is a mini-bomb. A few precautions will keep disaster at bay.

When I use an aerosol finish, I always open a window or a garage door and turn on a fan behind me to blow air across the ventured out the window.
The flow of fresh air keeps the fumes from getting in my face. I also wear a good organic vapor respirator.

While these precautions keep me from inhaling the vapors, they do not affect overspray sticking to everything in its path.

My solution is to spray small projects inside a large cardboard box with a furnace filter. This simple disposable booth collects excess spray Aerosol finishes have varying shelf lives:

It is almost indefinite for lacquer and shellac, but varnish driers lose their effectiveness after about two years. A sample spray is recommended with any can of finish that is unknown in age to ensure proper drying.

The key to getting even coverage is to keep your wrist locked. Keep the can 6 to 12 inches away from and parallel to the workpiece low on your wrist to move the can in an arc.

"If it works, don't mess with it," is a common refrain among woodworkers when it comes to finishing. Learning a new finishing technique can be difficult and confusing.

So, it appears to be easier to stick with an old standby like tung oil varnish, even if it is only adequate. If this is your practice may have overlooked an important class of finishes: paint.
Paint is a versatile medium because it can be used as a design accent to emphasize a piece's lines or to draw attention to beautiful woods in furniture.

A painted finish also allows you to use up scrap wood that is "too good to burn." But don't be fooled. Poor workmanship or shoddy surfaces cannot be concealed by paint.

A painted finish necessitates more prep than a clear finish. Fortunately, there is some merchandise available that makes the entire procedure relatively painless. If I need to paint a large project or one that requires a specific color, I use good latex paint and an airless sprayer.

However, for the majority of items, particularly those that require a professional-looking paint job, I use ordinary aerosol spray cans for priming.

Clear coating and painting

Auto parties have a fantastic variety of colors and types to choose from. Also excellent are automotive fillers and putties. Due to the meticulous demands of car finishes, people working in the automotive industry are constantly refining paint finishes.

That's why I get many of my furniture-finishing supplies, such as fillers, primers, and paints, from my auto parts store. And, because the paint is more easily scratched and difficult to repair than most clear finishes, I use another technique borrowed from automobile finishers: I clear coat my painted finishes. Before I invest in anything, I plan out my entire painting strategy.

Painting, like any other finishing technique, can be aggravating when an unexpected issue arises halfway through the process.

Testing all of your materials and practicing new techniques on scrap wood is the best way to avoid surprises.

After all, you wouldn't cut dovetails for the first time with valuable wood. As a result, you should approach paint finishing in the same manner.

Before cutting the first board for a piece of furniture, paint decisions must be made. Because my furniture pieces frequently incorporate painted, stained, and clear-coated elements, it's easier to finish each component separately and then assemble them.

However, careful building planning and final assessment are required. The elimination of complex masking results in better finish results. Consider which components will require special consideration when selecting stock for your venture. For example, if you decide that certain parts must be extremely smooth, maple, poplar, and birch are excellent wood choices.

However, if you want to show some wood texture through the paint, open-grained woods like oak and ash are better choices.

Smooth, glossy black coffee table legs would complement the mahogany veneer top and apron.

Also, if you want the legs to be tough to protect them from knocks, maple is the obvious wood choice. However, as far as painting goes, the wood used is irrelevant, as long as you are cautious with the under-under-paintings

Surface preparation is critical to achieving flawless painted furniture. Minor flaws that would otherwise go unnoticed under a clear finish are dramatically magnified by the monochromatic nature of the paint.

Before painting, small tear outs, hairline cracks in knots, stray sanding scratches, and other seemingly minor flaws must be filled and smoothed.

This may appear to be a lot of tedious work, but by following car surface preparation steps, you can reduce the labor.

Chapter Twenty Six

Sanding and Priming

All parts should be thoroughly sanded and inspected under a bright light before filling any voids with auto-body fillers.

Bondo and White Knight are two polyester filler brands that work exceptionally well for repair because they adhere tenaciously to raw wood, cure quickly, and sunnily, and accept most types of oil-based and latex primers and paint.

Most importantly, they do not shrink. They have a bad odor and a short working life once blended, usually less than 15 minutes.

Fill dents and nicks in coffee table legs with a two-part auto-body filler. I even repaired a band saw edge that had been clipped.

In addition, I filled in the knots. Knots, no matter how sound they appear, always have cracks that show through the paint. Knots frequently contain resins, particularly in softwoods.

So, after the filler in the knots cured for about 30 minutes, I sanded it flush and spot-sealed the knots with shellac to be safe.

Finally, I used spackle to make the edges of the medium-density fiberboard top perfectly smooth. Because I don't have a paint booth in my home shop, I set up a crude but effective painting area in my garage before priming or painting.

A box fan draws outside air through an open rear door and exhausts it through a partially opened garage door to provide ventilation for my plastic spray booth.

I also wear a good organic-vapor respirator when spraying primer and high-solvent lacquers from aerosol cans.

Primers serve the same functions as sealers under clear coats in painted finishes. Primers keep resins and extractives in place to discolor the paint, create a uniform nonporous base for the color coat, and highlight any defects missed during the filling procedure

When painting small areas, aerosol primers are a good choice. Under pigmented lacquer paints, I frequently use automotive high-build, scratch-filling primers. High-build primers are simple to apply, sand well, and fill in small nicks and pits in wood.

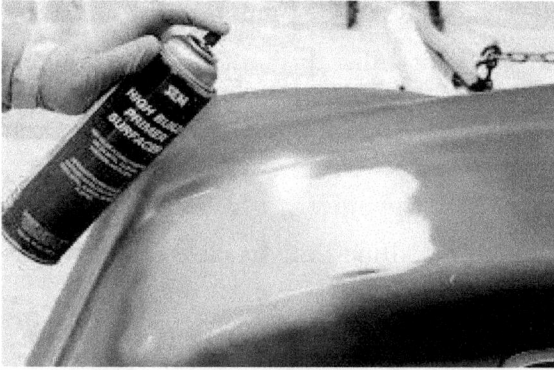

In my shop, adhesion tests show that automotive primers are completely compatible with high-solvent lacquers, but only marginally compatible with oil paints and not at all compatible with latex.

When I go to the store to buy primer, I grab several different brands of cans and shake each one until the little agitator ball falls out.

I choose the can that takes the longest to loosen the ball because this generally indicates that the primers contain a higher percentage of solids. Primers with higher solids perform better and are easier to sand.

Allow the primer to dry thoroughly so that it powders easily when sanded, and then carefully inspect the piece.

You'd be surprised at how many imperfections will appear on your supposedly smooth wood.
You must fill in the small flaws or they will show through the paint. However, do not use the two-part auto filler this time because it will not adhere to the prime coat.

Instead, use automotive glazing putty, which is designed to be applied over primer. Glazing with Acryl-Blue Putty is ideal for my needs, but any non-shrinking brand should suffice.

Smooth out the primer and dried putty. After that, apply one more coat of primer. Then sand once more. This time, sand to a minimum of 220 grit but no finer than 320 grit.

Be careful not to cut through to the wood while sanding, or you will have to re-prime. The goal of this final sanding is to level and smooth the surface while still leaving some small scratches in the primer. This slight texture, known as a tooth, improves the bond between the primer and the top coat.

Chapter Twenty Seven

Clear Coating & Rubbing Out

Aerosol paint cans come in a variety of colors, gloss levels, and brands. I've had good results with Plastic-Coated and Kyron on furniture.

Low-gloss aerosol paints sand easier than high-gloss paints, but I prefer the high-gloss variety because the higher resin content adds to the finish's resilience.

However, you shouldn't be too concerned about the actual glossiness because the final sheen of the project will be controlled by the clear coat. To begin painting, I neglected to apply a tack coat of paint over the entire primed area.

Then I spray several light coats to fill in the gaps until the entire surface has a level wet coat. Continuing to paint at this point will result in runs or sags.

Allow the solvent to evaporate for about 5 minutes before applying another coat in the same manner. On a well-primed substrate, two or three coats are usually sufficient to provide adequate color build.

I overcoat the spackled and sanded edge of the tabletop with the same automotive primer and paint that I used on the legs. The only difference was that I masked off the top and then held the work on a lazy Susan.

The clear coat is the finishing touch that distinguishes a standard paint job from a true showstopper. Clear coats not only protect the paint from dings and scratches but also add depth to the finish, making it more suitable for fine furniture.

Furthermore, clear coats unify components by providing a consistent sheen throughout the piece. Clear coats are also easier to remove and repair than paint.

To be safe, I usually choose a clear finish from the same resin family as the paint. I used an aerosol auto motive clear acrylic as my medium. I used Pratt & Lambert clear coat to protect the tabletop edges. To achieve a good film thickness, four or more clear coats may be required.

Remember that when rubbing out, some film will be lost, so account for this. Before applying the clear coat, make sure your paint is completely dry. I prefer to wait a few days.

I like to use liquid auto-motive buffing compounds to buff out clear coats to a high luster. I've discovered that car buffing compounds are easier to use than those sold at most wood finishing supply stores. Both 3M and Maguire's make good polishing compounds.

Maguire offers a variety of formulas with varying abrasive levels for hand rubbing or power buffing. Allow the clear coats to dry for a day or two before buffing to the desired sheen.

My coffee-table top's MDF edges presented a unique finishing challenge for me. Because the top was veneered, I needed a way to conceal the MDF core.

The solid wood edge banding was an option, but it didn't work with my design. Because of the fashioned edge that I desired, I ruled out veneer as well. So, like the legs, I decided to paint the edges black.

But first, I had to prepare the MDF surface for primer. MDF soaks up the finish like a sponge, and small pits in the core must be filled or the paint will show through. Some finishers address this issue by applying glazing coats; this technique requires considerable skill.

Large furniture manufacturers solve the problem by spraying on a two-part edge filler or surfacer, but it is expensive, difficult to find, and time-consuming specialized spray tools are required I avoided all of this by spackling the exposed MDF edges with a wallboard spackling compound.

The spackle sands easily fill pits and provide a solid foundation for the primer. Mask off the top and bottom to save yourself some time. before you begin spackling the edge of the tabletop

Chapter Twenty Eight

Steps to Painted Finishing

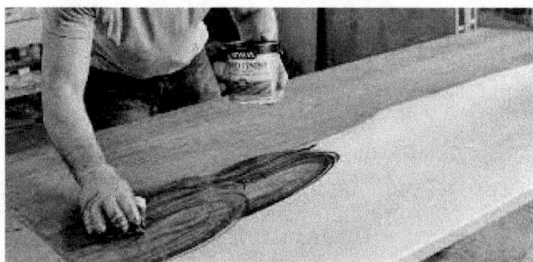

If the word paint conjures up images of a pail of house paint, a roller, and a brush, it may be difficult to connect it to fine furniture.

Nonetheless, painted built-in cabinets, bookcases, wall units, and furniture are as popular today as they have always been, and a good paint job rivals the best clear finish.

There's more to getting a good painted finish than meets the eye, and the process isn't the same as getting a clear finish. Much of the effort is focused on creating a perfectly flat, smooth base for the paint.

To achieve this base, I go through a series of preparation and priming steps that gradually smooth out the piece's surface.

Because the wood will be hidden beneath the paint, it makes no sense to use expensive furniture-grade hardwoods like oak, ash, walnut, and mahogany. Paintable woods include poplar, MDF, birch plywood, pine, and paint-grade alder and maple.

Paint grade simply means that the wood has variations in grain or color that make it unsuitable for a clear or stained finish.

Even though any repairs will be hidden beneath the paint, preparing the wood for painting is more important than preparing it for a clear finish.

The first step is to inspect all surfaces and fill any holes, cracks, or gaps, followed by removing any glue runs or drips. Sand the wood with PISO-grit paper after the filler has dried.

This grade of paper levels and uniformizes the surface while leaving it slightly rough so that the primer has some "tooth" to latch onto. Starting with any areas that were filled, sand each surface; excess filler will create a high spot that will show lip later in the finish.

However, the filler used in large holes may shrink, leaving a recess that must be filled and sanded again.

If you don't pre-treat the end grain, it will absorb a lot of primers. Seal the end grain with glue size, shellac, glazing putty, or spackle and then sand it smooth, or burnish the surface with P220 or higher grit sandpaper to prevent the primer from soaking in too deeply.

The goal with routed profiles is to achieve a smooth surface while retaining the profile's crispness. Automotive glazing putty dries too quickly, and glue size is difficult to sand; glue size, like shellac, does not fill the smallest voids that cause a rough texture.

Spackle is the best filler for profiles in my opinion because it is easy to use and shape when dry. Spackle is especially well suited for filling mitered corners in crown molding, where the detail and location necessitate a filler that can be easily spread and sanded.

The final step is to lightly sand the sharp corners, rounding them slightly. This step, known as breaking the corners, allows the paint to flow from a flat surface onto a corner, preventing paint buildup. It also reduces the possibility of sanding through the primer in the corners.

It's time to prime now that the obvious flaws have been filled, everything has been sanded, and the corners have been broken. Consider primer to be essential for achieving the flat, smooth base required for a painted finish.

Primer serves a variety of functions that either the paint does not or does not as well as primer. The first coat of primer may be unevenly absorbed. Apply a thin layer of primer.

Because MDF and maple are dense and free of pores, one coat of primer is frequently all that is required. Other woods typically require two coats, but three coats are not uncommon.

Despite the extra prep on end grain and profiles, these areas may still absorb an excessive amount of primer. The natural tendency is to apply it more heavily to achieve continuous, even coverage.

However, applying primer too thickly causes sags and runs, as well as slowing drying time. A better option is to apply a primer in several thin coats until uniform coverage is achieved.

When the primer has dried, it's time to find and repair any surface flaws that this first coat revealed. After the first coat of primer, every little hole, crack, and other imperfection that you missed during surface preparation stands out clearly.

CHAPTER TWENTY NINE

FILLING AND SANDING

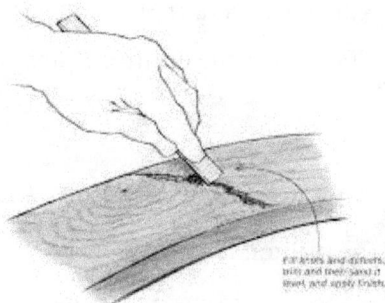

Fill dents and defects, trim and then sand it level, and apply finish.

If you need to make minor repairs and are using MDF or maple, sand the entire surface carefully after the filler has dried. On a sanding block or a random orbit sander, use P220 grit.

If the primer has soaked in thoroughly, or if there is a strong grain pattern, the entire surface will require vigorous sanding, which may result in the removal of the majority of the primer.

If the grain is visible, sand with P150 grit until either the wood shows through the primer or all of the shiny dimples on the surface disappear.

On large, flat areas, use a random orbit sander; on narrow boards, molding, or inside corners, use a sanding sponge.

Fold the sponge to fit the width to avoid cutting through the edges and corners of narrow pieces. After you've sanded everything, remove the dust and feel the surface with your fingers.

Sand any rough spots again as needed. If there are any bare spots, prime and sand them once more. Then, over the entire surface, apply a second coat of primer.

Sand this extra coat with P220 grit paper and a fine sanding sponge, taking care not to cut through the primer.

When finished, remove the dust and inspect the surface to ensure that all problem areas have been addressed.

The surface should be as free of flaws as you want the final painted finish to be. If you sanded down to the bare wood, prime and sand only those areas again.

It's time to paint now that all of the hard work has been completed. If you haven't sanded the primed surfaces in more than a day, go over them quickly and lightly with P220 grit sandpaper.

Because primer, like other finishes, cures for several days, sanding scratches tend to shrink and close, reducing the bond between primer and paint.

If the paint is tinted and you have more than one can, combine them in an empty paint bucket to ensure a consistent color throughout the job. Then, until half full, pour the paint into a smaller container with a large opening.

Dip the brush into the paint only halfway up the bristles, then gently tap it against the inside wall to remove excess paint. Brush long strokes with the grain, holding the paintbrush at a 45-degree angle to the surface.

Overlap strokes to maintain a wet edge and use light pressure to keep all bristles in contact with the surface.

To avoid leaving a ridge, pull up as you reach the end of a stroke.
When painting long surfaces in sections, start a new section just beyond the last strip and brush back into the wet section. Pooling occurs when you begin in the wet section.

Attempting to achieve 100 percent coverage with a single coat encourages applying the paint too thickly. Scuff-sand between coats to ensure good adhesion, and allow the paint to dry for at least two weeks before putting the piece to use.

After the second coat of paint has dried for 24 hours, apply a coat of clear finish for added resilience, depth, and optional sheen adjustment.

The amount of sanding required before the clear coat is determined by the texture of the painted surface and the final sheen. If the surface is flat and you intend to use a satin or semi-gloss clear coat, a light scuff sanding is sufficient.

If there are significant brush ridges or if you want a high gloss, sand the paint until it is level. Sand by hand with

sponges for sanding Their padding prevents them from cutting through the paint.

Miraka's Arlon abrasive pads can be attached to a random orbit sander to speed up the job on larger flat surfaces.

To minimize color changes, the clear coat should be completely clear, non-yellowing, and paint compatible. Water-based polyurethane is an excellent choice. You will be rewarded with a painted finish that is just as appealing as the best clear finish.

1 - Planning:
Fillers under a painted finish don't have to blend in, but they shouldn't shrink as they dry, leaving a low spot that needs to be filled. Sand table fillers should be used.

I also prefer quick-drying fillers. Some of the finest painted finishes can be found on automobiles, and auto-supply stores sell fillers that will help you achieve such quality. Automotive spot and glazing putty work well for fine cracks, flat end grain, and flat MDF edges.

Spackle works well on flat or routed end grain and MDF profiles. However, spackle should not be used to fill a large hole because sanding it will leave a depression on the piece's surface.

Spackle dries much slower than other fillers, so use it sparingly. A rough, porous surface is exposed when MDF is cut or routed. Covering the area with a spackle and then using a small, dampened brush with bristles is the best way to fill and smooth it.

Cut short to get the excess spackle out of the corners and curves before it hardens. When the spackle has dried, smooth it with a sanding sponge that has been shaped to fit the profile.

On MDF, avoid using a water-based primer, which can cause the fibers to swell and leave a bumpy surface Choose an oil-based primer or alcohol-based shellac instead.

2 – Primer:

Choose a primer that is compatible with the top coats and adheres well to both the wood and the top coats. The primer should also fill the grain, leaving the surface flat, and dry quickly and easily.

Choose a 100 percent acrylic primer if you intend to use a water-based top coat. In some cases, a different type of primer is preferred.

Shellac is an excellent choice for areas prone to stainings, such as wood knots, sap streaks, tannins, and pitch.

Use clear shellac to simply seal the wood, but pigmented shellac, such as Zinsser's BIN, to seal and prime the wood. If the paint you're using contrasts significantly with the white primer, tint the primer to a color similar to the paint.

With fewer coats, the paint will obscure the tinted primer, and if the finish is scratched or otherwise damaged, the primer will be less visible.
When I'm painting a piece of wood that will be stained or clear-coated, I use a clear sealer.

When primer or paint is applied to bare wood, it is difficult to remove every trace of the pigments; when the sealer is applied, it is easier to remove every trace of the pigments.

Water-based shellac, such as Target Coatings' Ultra-Seal, is an alternative to alcohol-based shellac. It is safe to spray and cleans up with warm, soapy water.

3 – Painting:
Interior cabinetry and furniture paint should be formulated to resist sags and runs, and it should dry quickly to prevent excessive dust collection. It should also provide a completely opaque finish after two coats and be durable enough for the piece's intended use.

Don't be tempted to save money by purchasing a $10 can of paint from a home center; quality is determined by price, so expect to pay upwards of $50 per gallon for paint used by professionals.

There are several high-quality acrylics and acrylic-enamel house paints available. Enamel is a generic term used by manufacturers to describe any paint with a smooth, hard surface.

To each gallon of paint, add a few ounces of Flotel, a latex paint additive that improves flow-out and leveling. A good brush is as important as good paint.

Pay a little more for a high-quality nylon brush with flagged ends. Nylon is softer than polyester or polyester blends, so the paint will lay down more smoothly with fewer brush-stroke ridges.

Flagged ends will result in a finer, smoother pattern. Spraying is the most efficient and convenient way to achieve a smooth, high-quality finish.

I use high-volume, low-pressure (HVLP) spray tools and paint designed for spraying. Target Coatings and M.L. Campbell are two good brands.

Chapter Thirty

Filling and Sanding

A glazed finish appeals to me. It gives the wood color and depth. As a result, I developed a simple glazing technique using polyurethane varnish.

I can create a long-lasting, hard finish that is resistant to heat, moisture, and solvents by using polyurethane varnish.

It is easily wiped on, which is a great benefit for anyone without spray equipment, I use a clear, satin, gel-polyurethane varnish based on mineral spirits.

Bartley makes a good one called "gel varnish." Aside from great depth, there are several other compelling reasons to use a glazed finish to color wood.

It's an excellent way to darken light-colored sapwood areas in a board. Then, depending on your preferences, you can darken or lighten the entire venture. Spotty areas can also be blended out.

Finally, glazing can be used to tame any wild grain, and it's nearly foolproof. There aren't many hard and fast rules with this technique, so each step can be customized as needed to achieve the desired finish color and depth.

Typically, bare wood is sealed with a sealer coat of thinned shellac. Then, depending on the color you want, a coat of stain can be applied. The glazing coats come next, usually one to three, but more can be used.

These colored coats are occasionally the same color but the colors of each coat are usually changed as needed to achieve the final color. A clear top coat is applied as a final step to help protect the glaze. Mix in Jap colors, universal tints, or even artist's ocularists to add color to a gel-polyurethane finish.

The majority of oil-based paints will also work. However, do not mix more than one part coloring agent with eight parts gel-polyurethane to avoid drying issues.

Another good option, which I used for the porringer table, is to incorporate one of Bartley's gel-stain merchandise. Bartley's gel products can be mixed in any proportion. Matching the glaze to your desired colors, as you might expect, is a matter of trial and error.

When trying to nail down the color, working with small amounts is ideal. Also included are down notes on the proportions of gel and colored so that you can achieve the same color gain.

Another point here. It would be prudent to complete all of the final steps on a test board first. You'll be able to look at the test board and see if the final result is what you want.

If you are dissatisfied with the appearance of a glaze coat as it is being applied, simply wet a paper towel or rag with mineral spirits and wipe off the entire coat.

Then, with the slate clean, make color adjustments and try again. And the coat beneath will be unaffected. It may take several adjustments until you achieve the desired color

If I've learned anything about finishing, it's that the quality of the sanding procedure on bare wood can make or break the final product.

SO-grit sandpaper can be used to remove heavy mill marks. Use 100-grit paper first, followed by 120-grit paper for lighter mill marks. You could use an even finer grit, say 180 or higher, depending on the hardness of the wood and the richness of the finish you want.

After you've finished sanding, apply a wash coat of shellac to all the surfaces. The shellac prevents splotching and streaking of the stain.
Although dewaxed shellac works best, white or amber shellac can also be used. Remember that each coat of shellac adds color, usually a very light amber.

To make a 1-pound cut of hardwood, such as the cherry used in the porringer table, mix one-part 3-pound cut shellac and one part denatured alcohol. For softwoods, use a thinner mixture of one part 3-1b.-cut shellac and three parts alcohol.

Avoid overlapping the brush strokes as you apply the shellac. This prevents you from spreading too much shellac in one area.

After the shellac wash coat has dried, use 220-grit sandpaper to remove any nibs of crystallized dust and raised grain that has dried in the finish.

My go-to weapon here is dry silicon-carbide paper. Taking the extra time to get a nice, even wash coat will make subsequent coats of finish easier and more consistent.

Begin the coloring process now by applying light to a medium shade of stain. I used a single coat of Minmax golden oak stain to give the porringer table a yellow tint.

If I wanted a brown tint, I would have used Minmax provincial stain. But don't let what I do bind you. You can use any color of oil-based stain to get close to the desired color

However, if a stain isn't going to help you achieve the desired color, simply skip this step. Using a brush, apply the stain and then wipe away the excess with a soft rag.

Flood the wood with stains when working on a flat surface, such as a tabletop. Then, with the brush, work in the liquid before wiping it away with the rag. You can get rid of the stain in small or large amounts.

It's best to apply the stain to one section at a time for better control. Begin with the least visible area and work your way up to the most visible.

Finally, give stains plenty of drying time, especially alkyd stains, which require 24 to 48 hours to completely dry.

If you skip this step, you're just asking for problems with the subsequent polyurethane coats.

Chapter Thirty One

Apply Glaze Coats

After the shellac and stain coats have dried, you can begin the glazing process. The glaze is applied with a brush and then removed with a cloth pad.

Using a pad to wipe off the glaze allows for more control than a brush. A couple of pieces of an old cotton T-shirt can be used to make the pad.

After cutting one piece into a rectangle, a smaller piece is folded and placed inside the rectangle. When the rectangle is wrapped around the inner piece, the result is a nice, soft pad that fits comfortably in your hand, similar to a French polishing pad. The first coat of glaze serves as the foundation for all subsequent coats.

Subsequent coats simply add to the first. The secret to the glazing steps is to go slowly and work only one area at a time.

Brush on the glaze kind of thick and then, depending on the desired look, either wipe off just about all of it or leave most of it on. And don't try to get to the final color in one coat. Several lightly colored coats look better than one dark coat.

For the cherry porringer table, I used a single coat of Bartley's golden oak gel stain, wiping off the stain lightly with the pad. But you can collect any color oil-based gel stain you want. Or you can add color to a clear gel.

Sanding

After this and all subsequent coats of glaze have fully dried, you need to do a little light sanding to smooth out the tiny nibs left in the dried finish. This sanding step also helps level out any uneven brush strokes.

Sanding between coats has the added benefit of leaving a better surface for the next coat to grab. Unlike lacquer, polyurethane does notelet into the coat below it, so the sanding scratches create a foothold for the new coat.

I find that 400-grit to 1,000-grit wet sandpaper dipped in soapy water does a nice job. But it's vital to sand with a light touch.

The first coat is thinner than paper, so it won't take much sanding to cut rough it. Be sure to eliminate all of the sanding dust before you before the coat of glaze.

If you don't, the new glaze coat will trap the dust particles on the surface. A good going-over with a vacuum will eliminate most of the dust. Then wipe it down with a tack rag to pick up the rest.

Second coat

Once the first coat has been sanded, it's time to apply color to the gel. But before starting, you'll need to make another cloth pad, since there therein and wiping to do.

I wanted the porringer table to appear aged and weathered. The idea was to have the finish look almost dirty from many years of service.
And to do so, I needed a dark, almost black color.

Scored one-part Boc art Ardleys'll stain with one of rt Bartley's clear gels. Because this mixture is thick, I usually add thinner until it is the consistency of cake batter.

If the color of the wood is fairly consistent throughout, you can simply brush on the glaze and wipe it off as needed. Try not to apply it so heavily that you get raised brush marks.

It should descend smoothly and flat on the surface. If the glaze is globing up on the surface with streaky color, you may have applied too much. Consider using a lighter coat.

Thin the glaze with mineral spirits or Petrol if necessary to make the rag glide smoothly. However, keep in mind that thinning the polyurethane mixture will also dilute the binding properties.

As a result, it will not adhere as well to the previous coat. As a result, don't mix more than one part glaze with one part thinner. If you want to even out the light and dark areas, use the glaze to darken the light areas.

Then decide how much glaze, if any, to apply to the dark zones. If you don't like the color as it's being applied, simply wipe it away with a paper towel or rag dampened with mineral spirits.

After that, change the color and try again. Allow each coat to dry completely. If you don't, and you need to remove the next coat, you may have to remove both coats instead of just one.

A glaze coat will dry overnight in most parts of the country, but in humid areas, I usually wait a little longer.

Additional coats of glaze

The lengthy drying time between coats has one advantage.

It gives you plenty of time to examine the changing color and depth of the finish and decide whether the next glaze coat's colors should be darkened, lightened, or changed entirely.

In most cases, the first coat of glaze, plus two or three additional coats, will be enough to achieve the desired color and depth. I applied two coats on top of the first coat for my porringer table.

A clear top coat will add depth to the layers of colored finish. Furthermore, the top coat provides a little more scratch resistance. I like to use Delft's polyurethane finish for small projects.

It comes in a spray can for easy application and has a thin consistency that makes it look less thick after drying.

On projects that are too large to be completed with a spray can, I use clear gel polyurethane thinned with Petrol to some extent. First, I thoroughly sand the surface with 1,500-grit paper dipped in soapy water. The gel is then applied with a clean cloth pad. I rarely apply a top coat to all of the surfaces of a project.

Instead, it is only used on large, horizontal surfaces that catch your eye quickly and stand out. As a result, only the tabletop on the porringer table received the top coat. I could stop here and be perfectly content with the results.

However, I prefer to add another step: buffing the finish. This step, like the top coat, is only used on tabletops and other horizontal surfaces. All that is required in this case is some buffing paste.

Finesse is a 3M product that I like. This product works best with an electric buffer and a wool polishing pad, but it can also be applied manually with a cloth pad.

Work on one section at a time. Begin by dabbing a small amount of the compound onto the tabletop, then buff it out with an electric polisher or cloth pad.

Finally, use a soft rag to wipe away any remaining compound on the surface. It's an excellent method for polishing the surface and bringing out all of the color and depth of your glazed finish.

Chapter Thirty Two

How to Use Wood Bleach

A move had damaged my friend's dining table, and two of its leaves were missing. The 50-year-old French-style reproduction table was veneered with a fruitwood that had the grain and texture of cherry.

The wood, however, had mellowed to a yellow-gold color. Cherry was an obvious choice for the new leaves. However, the color would be far too red and would gradually darken.

I used bleach to solve the problem. It removed the cherry's natural color, leaving me with a neutral background to match the original with a dye stain. The bleach also stopped the darkening process in the cherry leaves, ensuring that the color of the table remained consistent. Matching old wood to new is just one use for wood bleaches.

Most finishers are aware that bleaches remove undesirable stains such as food, black water, and old dyes. Bleaches, on the other hand, can do a lot more.

They also even out tonal differences in different woods and create blond or pickled finishes. The key is knowing which bleach to use.

It helps to understand how wood bleach works for this. Bleaches are classified into three types for woodworkers: peroxide, chlorine, and oxalic acid.

All three work by changing the way wood molecules reflect light, resulting in a change in color in the procedure. However, each type of bleach is designed for a specific purpose; they are not interchangeable.

Ideally, bleach should remove color selectively, meaning that it should only remove the color you want and not the color of anything around it.

In most cases, you'll need to experiment, especially if you don't know the stain's composition.

Because most bleach is highly corrosive to skin and highly poisonous, you should always wear good rubber gloves, a dust mask if you're mixing dry bleach powders and safety glasses. These bleaches are typically sold as two-part solutions labeled A and B. Peroxide wood bleaches are available at most paint and hardware stores.

Typically, the two compounds are sodium hydroxide and a strong hydrogen peroxide solution.

When used together, they produce a powerful oxidizing reaction that effectively removes the natural color of the good Peroxide bleaches will lighten some woods that have been treated with pigment stains to a lesser extent.

They do not affect dye stains. The most common way to use this product is to thoroughly wet the wood with sodium hydroxide (part A) and then immediately apply hydrogen peroxide (part B).

Part A must not sit for too long before applying part B to tannin-rich woods like cherry and oak, as the sodium hydroxide may darken the wood.

You can also combine the two parts and apply them simultaneously, as long as you do so quickly after the parts have been blended.

A single application is usually sufficient, but a second application may be required to even out the bleaching effect.

Peroxide bleaches do not affect some dark woods, such as ebony. If you want to bleach a tabletop with ebony inlay, you can take advantage of this.

If the bleach is applied unevenly to some woods, particularly walnut, a greenish tinge may appear in some areas.

To avoid this problem, apply the bleach sparingly, only enough to wet the wood. Don't saturate the surface.

After the wood has dried, use a weak acid, such as white vinegar, to neutralize the alkaline effect of peroxide bleaches. One part vinegar to two parts water is recommended.

After that, rinse with clean water. Peroxide bleaches will remove all-natural color variations in wood, so use them with caution.

I use them to match sun-bleached wood or as a neutral foundation for a decorative finish like pickled oak.

You can also use them to compensate for heartwood or sapwood variations, but I usually prefer to hand color or spray the sapwood with a dye stain to bring it in line with the heartwood.

Chlorine is a powerful oxidizer that will remove or lighten the majority of dye stains. Clorox or other weak chlorine-based laundry bleach will work, but it may take several applications to be effective.

Swimming pool bleach, a dry chemical called calcium hypochlorite, can be used to make a much stronger solution. It is inexpensive and can be purchased from a pool supply store.

The primary benefit of chlorine is that it will remove or lighten the dye without affecting the natural color of the wood.

You can use laundry bleach or the stronger version, dry calcium hypochlorite powder dissolved in hot water.

To make a saturated solution, dissolve the powder in water until no more powder dissolves. Only combine in glass or plastic containers: The chemical will corrode aluminum and steel.

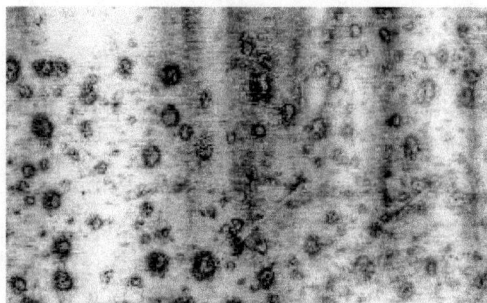

Because the mixture loses effectiveness when stored, I only make what I'll use right away. Before using, cool the room temperature and filter out solids. Apply the solution liberally to the wood, and the dye should disappear almost immediately.

Some dyes may take longer to bleach, while others may only lighten rather than disappear. Wait 24 hours to see the full bleaching effect. More bleach will not help if the color has not changed after two applications.

You'll have to try another method. On pigment-based stains, chlorine bleaches are usually ineffective. These can only be removed by sanding or scraping.

When iron and moisture come into contact with tannic acid, oxalic acid will remove a specific type of stain for the med.

Tannic acid is naturally present in some woods, such as oak, cherry, and mahogany.

When tannic acid reacts with water containing trace amounts of iron, it produces a black stain. Oxalic acid will remove the discoloration while preserving the natural color of the wood.

Oxalic acid also reduces the greying effects of sunlight. Some deck brighteners contain it as an active ingredient.

When used on furniture that has been stripped for refinishing, it will lighten the color and restore the wood's even tone.
Iron-based stains are relatively easy to identify. They are grayish-black in color and are usually fashioned into rings. They may also appear as a splotchy appearance on stripped oak.

Remove any finish before applying oxalic acid. In a plastic container, combine a solution of dry crystals of oxalic acid in hot water (available at most woodworking supply stores).

Allow the solution to cool to room temperature before applying it to the entire surface rather than just the stain. Several applications with overnight drying in between may be required.

After the wood's surface has dried, any residual oxalic acid must be removed before sanding or finishing, as the acid will damage subsequent finishes.

Several water rinses will remove the majority of the oxalic acid crystals that remain on the wood surface.

Use a solution of one quart of water and two heaping tablespoons of baking soda to neutralize the acidic wood surface. The Water should be used to rinse the baking soda solution.

The composition of stains that form on wood during the drying process varies. Common stains include sticker stains, brown stains, streaking, and light "ghost" stains.

Some can be removed with bleach. Because the stain's composition can be chemical or biological, removing a stain may require a trial-and-error approach. I frequently begin with oxalic acid and then add chlorine.

Peroxide bleaches are only used as a last resort because removing or lightening the stain can result in bleaching the surrounding wood.

Chlorine bleach can remove stains from grape juice, tea, and fruits. To achieve an even effect, remember to wipe the entire surface.

Some blue and black inks with iron bases can be removed with oxalic acid, but carbon-based inks, such as India ink, cannot be removed with any bleach.

When molecules selectively reflect light, color develops in an object. These colored molecules can be organic, like those found in dyes, or inorganic, like those found in pigments.

Most bleaches, such as peroxide and chlorine, work by interfering with the way molecules reflect light. Other bleaches, such as oxalic acid, convert a stain's-colored compound to a different, colorless compound.

The physics of these concepts may be difficult to grasp, but the important thing to remember is that bleaches do not truly remove a substance's color. They simply alter the material to make it appear colorless. Tannic acid and ferrous sulfate, for example, are colorless solutions when dissolved in water.

When the two compounds are combined, they react to form a third compound, iron tannate, which has a grayish-black color. tannate of iron is the compound that causes the majority of black water spots on oak.

When oxalic acid is added to this liquid, the colored iron tannate molecules are converted to iron oxalate, a colorless compound. Oxalic acid is bleached and used in this manner.

It is not possible to bleach every colored object. Colors produced by inorganic molecules will not be affected by bleach.

Many pigments, such as carbon black (used in inks) and earth pigments (used in wood stains), are unaffected by bleach.

Only by scraping or sanding the color off the surface of the wood can these colors be completely removed.

Chapter Thirty Three

Polished Finish Techniques

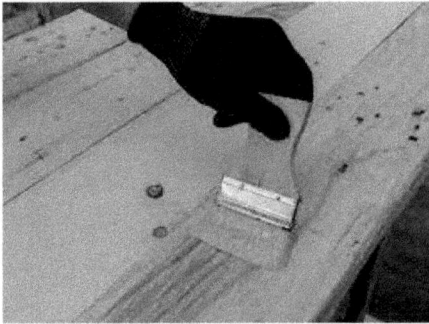

The basic idea behind rubbing out a finish is simple: Abrade the surface with fine sandpaper to remove surface defects and level it out, then polish it to the desired sheen.

The traditional method is to do this work by hand, with pumice and rottenstone, which works well but is time-consuming and physically exhausting.

Some modern products greatly simplify and accelerate this process. When combined with power sanding and buffing tools, these items provide an effective system for rubbing out a finish.

I prefer to wet-sand small surfaces by hand, such as table aprons and legs. For larger areas, such as tabletops, I use air-powered tools.

The best wet-sanding tools have opposing, in-line pads that vibrate back and forth in a straight line rather than creating a circular scratch pattern.

Some finishes, such as oil-based polyurethane and lacquers, can be dry-sanded with an electric random-orbit sander.

As long as you use very fine, 1,000-grit or higher standard papers or non-loading papers.

Electric sanders should never be used when wet-sanding due to the risk of electric shock. Begin the procedure with the finest grit size to remove defects and level the finish.

If the surface is badly orange-peeled or has ridges from brush strokes, start with 320-grit paper.

If you only have minor surface imperfections and want a glossy finish, you can start with 800-grit or even 1,000-grit paper.

I usually start with 400-grit or 600-grit silicon-carbide wet or dry sandpaper and lubricate all of my oil or lacquer-based finishes with mineral oil cutting 50 percent with mineral spirits.

I use a plant mister to spray the mixture. Some people would rather use water than oil. If you use water, lubricate it with a small amount of dishwashing liquid.

Working around the edges of a tabletop first, then toward the center, helps me keep track of where I am, working in sequence up to at least 600-grit paper.

If you want a glossy finish, use at least 800-grit or 1,000-grit paper. Sanding with a finer grit will expedite the polishing process later on.

Steel wool and Wool-Lube, a rubbing lubricant made by Behling, or thinned wax produce the best results for a classic, hand-rubbed satin finish.

Squeeze a few stripes of Wool-Lube onto the surface, then mist them with soapy water.

To remove the mineral oil from the wet sanding procedure, I mix a capful of dishwashing liquid into a quart of water.

Pushing down on a bathroom Cale with moderate downward pressure, about 25 Ibs., rub the surface in straight strokes with the pad, following the direction of the grain.

Repeat several times, then switch to a clean part of the steel-wool pad and rub the entire surface down again. Check your progress by wiping away the slurry.

When backlit, the surface should look like brushed metal if you did it correctly.

If you want a high gloss, automotive compounds, which are available at auto supply stores, are a real innovation for polishing furniture finishes. Compounds are simply abrasive powders suspended in liquids or pastes.

Meguiar's and 3M both make products that work exceptionally well on wood finishes.

They are used in stages to remove wet sanding defects and scratches. Some companies sell a single product that breaks down into smaller grits as you use it, but I prefer to use multiple compounds.

Because compound grit sizes vary, stick to products from a single manufacturer. Some buffing compounds can cause a whitish, hazy appearance on water-based lacquers. You may simply need to wait longer for the finish to cure, but the haze is usually caused by solvents in the compound that sometimes make the lacquer difficult to polish. If this occurs, stop using the compound and replace it with another.

As a final polish for water-based finishes, I've found that Meguiar's 10 plastic polish works well. Most rubbing compounds can be applied by hand, but a power buffer is recommended for large surfaces such as dining room tables. Right-angle sanders and polishers are the most commonly used buffers.

Get a variable-speed buffer or a two-speed tool if you buy one (rated at a maximum speed of 3,800 rpm). A locking nut secures a polishing bonnet made of cotton or synthetic foam to the butter.

Any bonnet can be cleaned, but to ensure efficient polishing, buy a separate bonnet for each compound grade.

Wear an apron and polish the furniture in an area where flying compounds will not be an issue. Apply a few stripes of the compound to the surface, about 8 in. apart.

Smear the compound over the surface of the finish while the buffer is turned off. Hold the butler at a slight angle off the surface, then turn it on and begin moving it slowly across the finish's surface.

Move the buffer about a foot every three to four seconds, working from the edges toward the center. When polishing edges, use smooth, confident strokes and pay attention to the angle and rotation of the butler.

They may catch the pad, resulting in a kickback. The sanding scratches disappear, and it's easy to tell when you're done with the compound.

Errant scratches will be highlighted by good overhead or backlighting. Apply finer grits to the first compound until a deep gloss appears. Allow the compound to dry before wiping it away with a soft cloth.

Some finishers use a glaze that contains silicone or another type of oil or polymer emulsion to fill in the tiny hairline scratches.

However, I usually finish with the 9-swirl remover, first with the buffer on slow speed, then by hand. I apply a small amount to a soft cloth and polish the surface by hand.

CHAPTER THIRTY FOUR
DECORATIVE FINISHING TECHNIQUES

The decorative painting dates back to around 3000 BC, when artisans in Egypt, India, and the Orient used marbling, grain stenciling, and other techniques to transform ordinary materials and objects into monumental works of art.

Along with more traditional trading route prizes, decorative painting techniques were brought to the West, where they have cycled in and out of fashion over the centuries.

Stenciling, in particular, was popular among North America's early colonists. Colonial furniture makers used stencils to decorate their low-cost chairs, and low-income homeowners stenciled their rough floors and plaster walls to mimic the beauty of the wallpaper and rugs they couldn't afford.

During the Victorian era, artisans in the United States and around the world were inspired by the Crafts Movement, elevating faux or false finishes—marbling and graining—to the realm of high style.

A pot of glaze and a feather in the hands of an expert can transform plain tabletops and small boxes into rich marble look-alikes; a deftly wielded graining brush can give plain pine furniture the luxurious look of walnut burl.

While stenciling techniques and materials changed little over time, the marbling and graining Techni of que ology became increasingly refined.

Close-mouthed professionals kept their trade secrets close to their vests, even carrying the details of their artistry to the grave.

Although novices may not be able to replicate the masters' finishes, pleasing results are usually attainable with a little patience.

Over an impervious base coat, the glaze is brushed, ragged, combed, sponged, or even pattered.

Except for stenciling, the color of the base coat is visible through the glaze in all decorative finishes, giving the finish a deep, subtle glow.

Because it is nearly impossible to match such a finish exactly, it is generally a good idea to mix more glaze than you think you will need. The patterning of the glaze is the true challenge of decorative painting. Stenciling is the simplest technique. Simply stipple the color on top of the base coat with a brush or a sponge while working through a paper or acetate template.

Marbling and graining are more difficult to achieve because the color and pattern must be reasonably realistic for the finish to be appealing..

This means that in marbling, you must first create a convincing cloud of background colors before shooting it through with natural-looking veins.

Graining requires even more skill than disguising as marble because the patterns of heartwood and sapwood are less free-flowing than the veins in marble.

Finishing will go more smoothly in both cases if you keep referring to a sample of the material you're trying to simulate.

Always test the appearance of the glaze over the base coat before beginning work on any decorative finish; with marbling and graining, practice patterning on large pieces of illustration board until you are confident in your technique.

Chapter Thirty Five

Stenciling Techniques

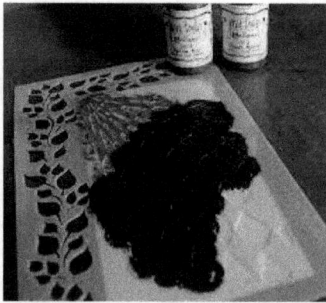

The decorative painting dates back to around 3000 BC, when artisans in Egypt, India, and the Orient used marbling, grain stenciling, and other techniques to transform ordinary materials and objects into monumental works of art.

Along with more traditional trading route prizes, decorative painting techniques were brought to the West, where they have cycled in and out of fashion over the centuries.

Stenciling, in particular, was popular among North America's early colonists. Colonial furniture makers used stencils to decorate their low-cost chairs, and low-income homeowners stenciled their rough floors and plaster walls to mimic the beauty of the wallpaper and rugs they couldn't afford.

During the Victorian era, artisans in the United States and around the world were inspired by the Crafts Movement, elevating faux or false finishes—marbling and graining—to the realm of high style.

Since the Egyptians began decorating mummy cases with stencils in ancient times, such decorative patterns have been a common feature of furniture design.

They have appeared on a variety of items ranging from shields to chairs and toy chests.

A stencil, which can be as simple as a finely veined leaf or as complex as a multicolored, repeating motif of fruits and flowers, can be applied to a piece of furniture either before or after the final coat of finish.

The stencil is typically scaled down or scaled up from a master Pattern and cut from a stencil board or acetate. Acetate is more durable than paper because it can be cleaned with mineral spirits and reused.

Most drafting supply stores sell translucent material. Stencil designs can be sprayed on or applied with special sentencing with a short bristle.

While early American settlers used milk paint to stencil, any thick-bodied paint, such as quick-drying Japanese colors or oil-based or acrylic paint, can be used. Acrylic paint will work just as well

Bronze powders can be combined in the same stencil to produce a range of metallic colors within a single design, creating the illusion of light and shadow—a technique made famous by the Hitchcock chairs of the mid-nineteenth century.

How to Make a Stencil
1 - Making a pattern larger

A photocopier with an enlargement feature can be used to create a larger version of a pattern for stenciling; another method is to transfer the shape using a grid.

Draw a grid of squares over the pattern, using a ruled straightedge to ensure that all squares are the same size. The pattern will be easier to redevelop if you make the squares smaller.

Make a larger grid on a blank sheet of graph paper or acetate, increasing the size of the squares by the same amount you want to enlarge the pattern.

For example, if you need a stencil design that is twice the size of the pattern, double the size of the second set of squares.

To create the stencil design, draw the part of the pattern that is in the corresponding square of the smaller grid in each square of the enlarged grid.

Follow the same steps to create a stencil that is smaller than the original pattern, but make the second grid smaller than the first.

2 - Making the pattern

Make a copy of your design on a piece of stencil board or acetate. Use carbon paper with the stencil board; for an acetate stencil, simply place the sheet over your design and trace it in ink.

Make a separate stencil for each color if your design will include more than one. Cut out the pattern with a swivel knife, pulling the knife toward you and keeping your free hand out of the blade's path.

Stenciling with Paint

1 - Taping the stencil down

To precisely align the stencil, draw a reference line down the center of both the workpiece and the stencil. Then, using masking tape, secure the stencil to the workpiece making sure the reference lines match up properly.

2 - Putting on the paint

Spray or brush on paint to transfer the stencil design to your work piece if you're spraying, use paper to mask the surfaces around the stencil and place the workpiece up on a work surface.

Holding the aerosol paint can 6 to 10 inches away from the workpiece spray the stencil until the exposed wood is lightly coated with paint above, and land left.

Keep the nozzle level with the stencil and spray in a straight line to prevent paint from bleeding under the stencil. Set the workpiece flat on a work surface and dip only the tips of the bristles in the paint to use a stenciling brush.

This will result in a light coat and thus less bleeding.
Holding the brush perpendicular to the surface, jab the bristles up and down on the stencil until the wood is completely covered, reloading as needed.

Allow each coat to dry before spraying or brushing on the next if you're using more than one stencil to apply multiple colors.

3 - Taking off the stencil

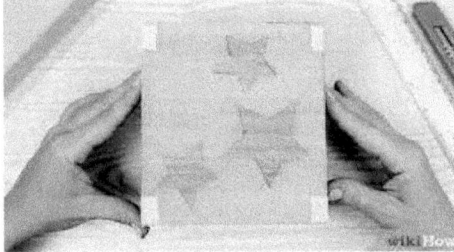

To avoid bleeding, remove the stencil while the paint is still wet. Remove the masking tape from two adjacent corners, then gently lift the stencil away from the workpiece pulling up the two sides evenly.

If you slide the stencil across the surface, you may smear some paint. After the parent has dried, use naphtha to remove any adhesive residue before top coating the workpiece

Stenciling with Bronze Powder

1 - Setting up the stencil

Cut out the pattern after drawing the stencil on acetate. Set aside the bronze powder in a bowl or on a palette. Apply a thin coat of slow-drying varnish to the surface you will be stenciling to prepare the workpiece to allow the varnish to dry until it is firm but tacky. Place the acetate workpiece piece with the glossy side down so that it adheres to the surface.

2 - Applying the powder

Wrap a piece of chamois or a clean, soft cloth around your index finger and dip it into the bronze powder while the varnish is still tacky. Rub the powder onto the surface exposed by the stencil cutouts.

Rub the areas you want to highlight hard; rub the areas you want to shade lightly. Apply more powder as needed until the surface is colored to your liking, but work quickly to prevent the varnish from drying completely before you finish.

Then remove the stencil. Apply several layers of bronze powder separated by thin layers of varnish to emphasize the three-dimensional quality. After you've finished stenciling, apply two final coats of varnish to protect the surface.

CHAPTER THIRTY SIX

STENCILING TECHNIQUES

Graining is the process of recreating the appearance of one type of wood on another for decorative purposes. The technique can be used to mimic the texture and warmth of more exotic species on species with muted grain.

Graining, on the other hand, can hide visual flaws, such as a wood patch used to repair a damaged surface.

You can develop a diverse range of styles, from the close grain of beech to the free-flowing pattern of pine, with practice, determination, and careful study of the species you wish to emulate. Graining was especially popular among westward-moving American pioneers in the 1800s.

Due to the scarcity of hardwood, woodworkers harvested softwoods and grained them to resemble more highly figured woods such as cherry, oak, and mahogany. Graining is done in stages. First, a flat base coat is applied to the surface and allowed to dry.

The grain pattern is then traced into the glaze with special graining tools such as combs and rollers before a color glaze is applied.

After that, a protective topcoat is applied. Graining glazes can be made in the shop, but commercial, ready-to-use glazing stains are just as effective; they can be tinted with Japanese colors to create almost any shade you want.

The glazes you make at home are usually one-part boiled linseed oil and two parts varnish, tinted with artists' colors.

A heavy-bodied consistency is required, but not so heavy that the drying time is prolonged, or the grain patterns will tend to flow back together. Special additives can be purchased to shorten the drying time.

1 - Glaze preparation and application
Tint a container of flat oil-based paint with the artist's colors matching the color of the wood you want to replicate.

Allow a layer of the paint to dry on your two work pieces and a base coat. Then, using a foam brush or a pad applicator, apply a graining glaze to the painted surface.

Wrap a soft cloth tightly around three of your fingers to begin the process of creating a grain pattern on the wood, then draw the cloth along the surface several times, drawing thin, wavy, parallel lines.

2 - Grainline refinement
Dip an artist's brush or a camel's hair sword striper in the glaze and draw slowly along the surface within the original lines to soften the grain lines from step 1.

Hold the brush at an angle to the surface for the best results. Rub in lines for a rough oval or diamond shape around where you will be adding the knot on your workpiece if you want to simulate a knot.
Experiment with the brush until the surface has the desired grain pattern.

3 - Inserting knots
Wrap a cloth around one fingertip and dip it in the glaze. Then, using a soft, dry brush, brush the surface back and forth in the direction of the grain to smooth out the patterns and blend them into the background.

This stage of the procedure is frequently ideal for a badger. Apply a topcoat after the surface has dried, and then polish it with rottenstone and paste wax.

Chapter Thirty Seven

French Polishing Techniques

French polishing is a time-honored finishing technique that involves padding shellac with a cloth. The result is a lustrous, almost three-dimensional finish characteristic of fine antique furniture.

Nonetheless, the look does not come easily. French polishing takes practice and a lot of elbow grease to master.

For most commercial woodworking shops, the labor time requirements rule out this type of finish; lacquers and modern spray tools are far more convenient.

Still, for an inexperienced woodworker, French polishing can be a rewarding way—some purists would argue the very best way—to complete a special project.

While the finish is not resistant to water, alcohol, or heat, it is relatively simple to repair once the piece has been completed. Wool and linen rags, pieces of old sweaters and shirts, or a well-washed bed sheet will suffice, shellac flakes, denatured alcohol, mineral oil, pumice, and polishing compound are all required for French polishing.

The amount of shellac in each gallon of alcohol is measured in pounds of shellac flakes dissolved. A 5-pound cut, for example, is 5 pounds of shellac dissolved in a gallon of alcohol.

We use a 2 to 3-pound cut for French polishing, whereas you will be dealing with quantities less than a gallon. The procedure consists of several steps that must be completed in the order listed below: On the first day, the wood is given a coat of oil and the excess is wiped away.

The pores are then filled with pumice. On the second day, additional coats of shellac are padded on to give the finish more body. The oil film is removed with a clean cloth on the third day.

This is the time to shine a light on the surface and build up the body. If you cannot afford the time required for French polish, padding lacquers can provide a similar look without the same level of effort. Padding lacquers are commonly used on old finishes, but they can also be used on new wood.

1 - Creating a pad

Fold the corners of a 3-inch square piece of wool toward the center, stretching the wool with each fold. After that, squeeze

Make an oval out of the wool pad and add a few drops of 2Vz- to 3t/pound cut shellac.

By crumpling the pad in your hand, distribute the shellac throughout the wool, and then place it in the center of a single thickness of coarse linen. Several drops of alcohol should be added to the pad.

2 - French polishing pad preparation

Gather the linen around the wool ball and twist it until the pad is securely in place.

Then, tap the pad against your palm to spread out the shellac and alcohol and create a flat surface.

Squeeze out any excess liquid if the pad is too wet. When not in use, keep the pad moist in an airtight container to keep it from stiffening.

3 - Pore enlargement

Allow a shellac sealer coat to dry after applying it with a brush. This procedure can be carried out before the creation of the pad. Then, sprinkle pumice on the workpiece and shake some on the pad.

Grip the pad tightly between your fingers and thumb, then work the pumice into the wood to find the most comfortable one.

Keep the pad moving while it is on the surface to avoid leaving a mark on the wood with the alcohol on the pad. Pay close attention to the edges to avoid leaving them unfinished.

As you rub the pumice, it will initially sound scratchy. The greater the filling of the pores, the less scratchy the pumice will sound.

Continue to pad, sprinkling on fresh pumice and adding more alcohol as needed, until the pores are filled and the surface is matte. This procedure may take 30 minutes or more, depending on the size of the workpiece Set the workpiece side for a day after filling the pores.

4 - Creating the film

To provide lubrication for padding the surface, prepare a new pad and dab a drop of oil onto it with your finger. Use the same strokes you used to fill the pores to polish.

With a wet pad, apply light pressure. Apply more pressure as the pad dries and the friction increases. Recharge the pad as needed with shellac and alcohol.

Repeat the procedure until the finish looks good to you and the polishing streaks are gone. Set the workpiece for a day. After the shellac has dried, the surface will have a milky clouding. This is the oil that was used to lubricate the pad; it has now risen to the surface and must be removed.

Soak a pad in alcohol and rub the surface in long strokes, or polish with a fine glazing compound, until the oil is gone. This will reveal the finished appearance of the French polish.

CHAPTER THIRTY EIGHT

MARBLING TECHNIQUES

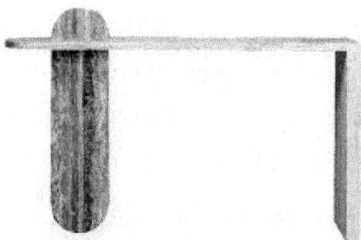

When structural constraints prevented the use of real marble, faux marble, or false marble, finishes were frequently used as a substitute on everything from walls and floors to furniture.

Real marble is formed as a result of intense natural forces that occur when limestone is melted under high heat and pressure. Minerals that flow through molten rock cool and crystallize.

Layers upon layers of veins in white, black, and other colors combine to form a lattice that is both opaque and translucent.

The majority of the techniques for recreating the look of marble on wood involve working with two or three colored paints on a wet, glazed surface. Rags, newspapers, and sponges are among the tools used to manipulate the paints. The finest tools for simulating the depth and pattern of the veins are fine brushes or a feather.

As a general rule, colors on a marbled surface should be limited to no more than three, including the base color. The color palette should be limited to the natural colors found in marble.

Marble's constituent parts flow during the stone's formation, and it is critical to capture this appearance of fluidity.

Work with good reference photographs or keep a sample of the real thing on hand to develop a realistic design.

1 - Putting on the glaze

Brush a coat of white, semi-gloss oil-based paint on your workpiece as a base coat and allow it to dry for the base coat of a white marble finish. Lightly sand the surface with 320-grit sandpaper to remove any brush marks.

Tint a small amount of white glaze with one of the artists' colors you'll be using in the finish.

Then, using a cloth or a creased piece of newspaper, apply glaze to the painted surface.

2 - Drawing in the veins of marble

Squeeze some of the artist's color used in step 1 onto a palette while the surface is still wet. Dip an artist's brush into the color and paint imitation-marble veins in the glaze with wavy strokes.

The veins should appear to wander around the surface randomly, forking right and left. A realistic effect can also be achieved by rolling the brush between your fingers while painting.

After you've finished painting all of the veins, remove any excess glaze by dragging a soft cloth diagonally across the surface.

Rep the procedure to add more marble veins in a different color.

If you want to add more veins, reverse the color order or mix them to add contrast and depth to the surface.

3 - Pattern smoothing

While the surface is still wet, gently stroke the veins with a soft, dry paintbrush such piece as a badger softener. Continue until the surface has a misty, translucent appearance.

Allow the surface to dry for 24 hours before applying a coat of semi-gloss or high-gloss polyurethane varnish. With a soft cloth, polish the two works

Making a marbled surface
1 - Draws broad veins

Spread a base coat of green paint and then a glaze tinted a lighter color on your workpiece or a green marble finish, following the procedure as described.

Dip the bird feather in the glaze and draw a diagonal line across the surface to create broad marble-like veins.

Smooth the pattern frequently by lightly brushing the veins with a marine sponge, badger softener, or a soft cloth.

While the surface is still wet, make another batch of glaze that is lighter in color than the first. Apply and feather this glaze in the same manner as the previous one, but this time, make the veins cross over the ones that are already in place.

2 - Unfolding the pattern

Dip a clean, stiff-bristled paintbrush into mineral spirits to create a mottled effect on the surface. Holding the brush a few inches above the workpiece runs a gloved finger along the bristles while spraying the veins with a fine mist.

3 - Finishing the pattern

To avoid blabbing, dip a bird feather in white artist color and let the excess drip off.

Then, with the feather tip, draw a series of thin white veins within the broad veins that are already on the surface. Smooth, varnish, and polish the surface once all of the fine veins have been painted.

CHAPTER THIRTY NINE

RUBBING TECHNIQUES

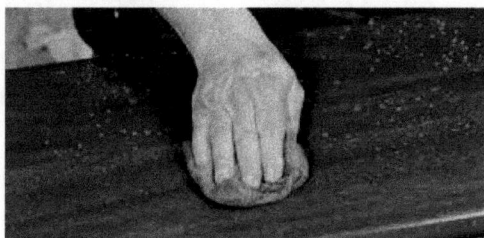

Although wormwood working analogs are brimming with rubbing compounds and fancy electric polishers, purists stick to the centuries-old method of "rubbing out" a finish with traditional abrasives.

Rubbing a satin sheen finish with pumice, a powdered form of volcanic rock gives the wood a soft look reminiscent of brushed brass and leaves it smooth and silky to the touch.

Taking the process, a step further with an even finer powder known as rottenstone eliminates the abrasions caused by the pumice to add an extra measure of shine—even to glossy topcoats of varnish or lacquer.

The idea of rubbing out a meticulously applied topcoat with abrasive compounds may sound strange. However, the final coat of finish on a piece of furniture is rarely clear and perfectly smooth.

It is common for the topcoat to be speckled with dust and dirt particles that settle on the finish before it dries. Furthermore, the tool used to apply the finish's signature may be visible.

Even when brushes are handled with care, they frequently leave behind faint bristle marks, and a sprayed surface may have the texture of an orange peel.

As a result, the first step in the rubbing procedure is to level the surface as precisely as possible. The smoother it is, the better the topcoat looks and feels. After leveling the surface, it can be buffed to almost any sheen.

The grit of the abrasive you use determines the difference between a rubbed satin finish and a buffed to a gloss finish. For example, rubbing compounds contain particles that leave minute scratches on a surface.

Coarser-grit compounds leave a fairly large pattern on the surface, making them appear dull or satin. Finer-grit compounds leave less visible marks, resulting in a glossier appearance. Rub out can be done with almost anything that abrades. Finishers use sandpaper, steel wool, and nylon abrasive pads in addition to rubbing compounds.

The size of the scratch pattern determines the level of sheen in each case. If there is an inherent issue with rubbing out, it is the risk of rubbing through the finish.

Because the procedure involves grinding small amounts of the thinly layered topcoat, the possibility of cutting through the coating to the wood exists.

You must exercise extra caution near the edges. Rubbing through even the top layer of some varnishes will result in a blemish.

The resulting outline of the cut area, known as a "halo" or "witness line," serves as a subtle but visible reminder of how thin each layer of a finish truly is. While the majority of the rubbing out procedure is material removal, the final step returns a small amount. Waxing a surface adds an ultra-thin layer of protection on top of the rubbed topcoat, imparting a little protection more sheen and tenacity to the finish.

You may be eager to move on to the next step after applying a final coat of finish to your workpiece and waiting for it to dry. However, before rubbing out a topcoat, it must first dry and set hard enough to be worked over with very fine abrasives.

Before rubbing out your workpiece you must wait for the topcoat to cure—that is, to become as hard as it will set.

You are more likely to scratch the finish during the rubbing-out phase if the finish has not had time to cure. No two finishes require the same amount of time to complete.

The length of the procedure is determined by several factors, including the type of finishing product used, the number of coats applied, and the amount of time between subsequent coats.

Shellac and water-based finishes, for example, can usually be rubbed out after 24 hours. Lacquer takes about 48 hours to dry, while varnish takes three or four days.

The curing time for oil finishes can be weeks. The more coats applied to a surface, the longer the curing time.

However, keep in mind that a finish cures faster if more time is allowed for drying between coats.

Before applying a finish, always read the instructions; a recommended curing time is usually indicated.
The sheen you achieve after rubbing out a finish is determined by the abrasives you use.

Use 400-grit paper to achieve a satin finish, then buff the surface. For a semi-gloss finish, combine 0000 steel wool with 400-grit paper. A high gloss can be achieved by using finer grit sandpaper, such as 600, in conjunction with a rubbing compound.

The same effect can be obtained by using 600-grit paper and pumice or rottenstone. Begin by sanding the topcoat down to a matte sheen. If you use wet or dry sandpaper, choose a finer grit than the one you used to prepare the surface for the final coat of finish.

The following step is to remove all dust and sanding particles, and then Repeat the abrading process several times with finer-grit papers. Stop at 400-grit paper for a dull or flat-looking surface. For a glossier finish, increase the grit.

To determine whether a topcoat has cured, perform the simple tests listed below. Try digging your fingernail into the finish on an inconspicuous area.

A component of the workpiece indentation should not be possible. If you do, the finish will require more curing time. Another good indicator is the smell.

If you can smell the solvent on the workpiece the topcoat is not ready to be rubbed out. After the finish has passed both of these tests, lightly sand a hidden area.

Allow more time for curing if the paper becomes clogged. The top coat is fully cured if the paper glides over the surface, turning some of the finish to powder.

There are two opposing schools of thought regarding the best way to sand a finish. The traditional method is to use a felt block to carefully work pumice and rottenstone over the top coated surfaces. A less hidebound technique employs one or more modern abrasives, such as rubbing compounds, steel wool, or sandpaper, and may even employ an electric polisher.

Both approaches have advantages. Working with pumice and rottenstone is time-consuming, but it earns the approval of woodwork purists.

The modern way is simpler and requires less effort, but some argue that it requires less craft. Both techniques are demonstrated on the following pages.

Whatever path you choose, remember that the finer the abrasive you use, the glossier the sheen you will achieve. You can achieve one sheen using either rubbing out technique.

By buffing the finish with wax, any luster can be enhanced. However, don't rely solely on the wax to increase the gloss; it won't transform a satin finish into a semi-gloss, for example.

Instead, the wax will only enhance what is already present. While all surfaces of a workpiece must are rubbed out, pay special attention to tops because they are the most visible features of most furniture. If you choose the traditional method, you must use a lubricant with pumice and rottenstone. The most common lubricants are water and oils such as paraffin and mineral oil.

Working with water has two advantages: it cuts pumice faster than oil, speeds up the process, and leaves no oily residue.

Using water on shellac, on the other hand, will turn the finish white. The traditional rubbing-out lubricant, paraffin oil, is a better choice for shellac topcoats.

Keep every stroke parallel to the wood grain when painting tabletops and other flat surfaces. Begin near a corner and move along the edge in a straight line, rubbing the surface with moderate pressure from one end to the other.

With each subsequent stroke, alternate directions until you reach the opposite edge. Keep the abrasive moving; the friction caused by rubbing a single spot for too long may burn the finish.

Avoid making arc-like strokes, which will highlight any scratches on the surface.

Use a shop-made rubbing pad that will follow the curves of your workpiece or rounded surfaces that are difficult to work with a rigid abrasive pad.

When working with pumice, use a short, stiff-bristled brush to sprinkle it on the surface. Then, wrap a sheet of sandpaper around a thick sponge that is small enough to fit in your hand.

As you rub the finish on the surface, wrap the paper around the sponge. Steel wool or a commercial rubbing pad can also be used on some types of finishes.

How to Remove a Rusted Finish

1 - Applying the lubricant: Dip your fingers in the lubricant and sprinkle several drops on the surface to be rubbed out.

If you're using oil as a lubricant, put on rubber gloves.

2 - Abrading the surface: Shake some pumice onto the surface, then lightly abrade it with a felt block. If you don't have a felt block, wrap a scrap of wood in burlap instead.

Continue rubbing the surface until a rottenstone-lubricant mixture forms. To inspect the finish, periodically wipe a small area of the surface with a soft cloth. You want to make sure you're not rubbing the topcoat off.

3 - Removing the pumice and lubricant: Using a clean cloth, wipe away the abrasive and lubricant. Examine the sheen on the surface; the finish should have a satin luster. You can either stop the procedure here or repeat it to achieve a glossier sheen.

Fit a buffing bonnet to the machine's polishing disc and coat it with wood rubbing compound. Begin near the center of the surface and work your way outward, moving the bonnet continuously.

Electric polishers work quickly, so stop the tool frequently and wipe a small area of the surface with a cloth to inspect the topcoat's condition.

When the surface has a satin appearance, you can either stop the procedure or continue with a finer grit rubbing compound to achieve a glossier luster.

Using a clean cloth, apply a small amount of rubbing compound to the wood surface. After you've abraded the entire surface, wipe the compound away with another cloth.

Repeat the procedure with a finer grit compound for a glossier sheen. Some finishers rub out the finish with a lubricant and super fine steel wool or a commercial rubbing pad to achieve a softer gloss than is possible with rubbing compound.

Waxing to provide a protective sheen
1 - Applying the wax: A wax coating will protect a rubbed-out topcoat from damage, but choose a product with denser consistency than a liquid or cream wax. Scoop a small amount of the wax onto a clean cloth, then apply a thin, even coat to the surface, rubbing it into one small area at a time.

If you work on too large a surface area at once, the wax's solvent may evaporate before you can rub it over the surface, causing the wax to harden prematurely. Allow the wax to dry for the time specified by the manufacturer, which is usually about 15 minutes.

2 - Buffing the wax: Using a clean cloth, rub the waxed surface until it is smooth. shines. For contours or detailed surfaces, buff the wax with a stiff-bristled brush, in short, brisk strokes.

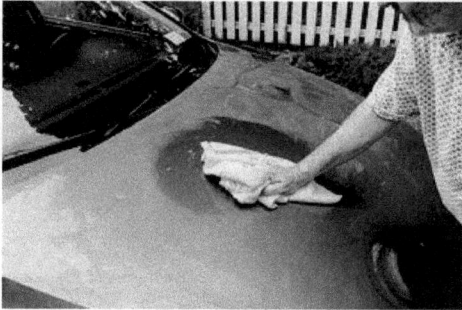

CHAPTER FORTY

PROTECTIVE FINISHING TECHNIQUES

In contrast to a cabinetmaking project, where wood is cut away until you are satisfied with the shape that will last, a finish is built up layer by layer.

Simply put, finishing is the process of applying a fluid to wood and allowing it to dry in thin sheets. While this is a slower and less dramatic stage of a project, the result is just as important in producing a beautiful piece of furniture.

The amount of protection provided by a finish is perhaps its most impressive feature. Most commercial finishes are no thicker than a book page, but they must protect the wood from dirt, moisture, and even mild abrasion. The earliest clear finishes were probably applied in the most basic way possible- wiped on with whatever was available.

A true oil finish is made up of nothing but natural drying oils were poured onto the wood. After wiping away the excess, a thin film is left to dry. After one or two coats of sealant, subsequent layers can be built up to almost any thickness or sheen.

Even today, the phrase "hand-rubbed finish" evokes images of luster and quality. Shellac, a naturally occurring resin, can be handled similarly to oil.

One or two coats will seal the wood, but you can continue to add coats to achieve the deep, glossy finish known as French polish.

Most topcoats can be applied by hand, and wiping is one of the best and simplest methods for ensuring thin, even coverage of a wood surface.

Wood absorbs finish at different rates due to its structure (under a microscope, it looks like a bundle of straws). When a finish is applied uniformly, it frequently appears to have uneven coverage.

Because the end grain absorbs more finish, its surface appears bare, whereas adjacent faces and edges appear adequately covered. The solution is to flood a coat of finish on the end and flat grain areas and allow different amounts to be taken in. When you wipe off the excess, the wood will be properly covered.

Finishers must have grown impatient with the thin coats that wiping produces over time, and brushes were introduced into the procedure.

Brushes allow you to get into the most inaccessible carvings and crevices, apply finish quickly in denser coats, and keep your hands clean.

With the various bristle types and brush configurations available today, there is a brush for nearly every type of finishing product.

With the invention of the spray gun in the 1920s, application times were further reduced.

Spraying a finish is by far the quickest method, blanketing the wood in a cloud of finely atomized fluid. However, technology has drawbacks.Spray guns can be wasteful because a large portion of the cloud generally misses its target.

One of the goals of finishing tool designers is to create a new generation of spray guns that maintain their traditional speed while reducing waste.

CHAPTER FORTY ONE

OTHER TOOLS AND ACCESSORIES

The application stage, like all other stages of a finishing project, will be aided by a few specialized accessories.

If you have the patience and energy to put in some elbow grease, you can color a surface with a variety of clothes, pads, and brushes. Cloths and pads made from old sheets or linen can be made and prepared in the shop; you can also make your foam brush. Brushes come in a variety of styles, sizes, and price points.

If you prefer bristle to foam diversity, a high-quality brush is a good long-term investment. It will outlast a cheap brush, but more importantly, it will produce a better finish.

On the market, there are two main types of spray systems. Until recently, the only available system included a compressor connected to a spray gun.

The more compact high-volume, low-pressure (HVLP) system is becoming more common today. The HVLP is less expensive to operate and less harmful to the environment because it produces less overspray and thus produces less waste.

Both spray systems must contain the fumes and safely exhaust them. If the workpiece is small enough to fit inside the booth, a commercial spray booth is a good option.

Chapter Forty Two

Choosing a Protective Finish

The protective finish you choose for the project is heavily influenced by your personal preferences and the effect you want to achieve.

Tung oil, for example, is notable for its ability to penetrate wood, imparting a warm glow to the surface and emphasizing grain and pattern. A varnish or polyurethane topcoat provides more protection by drying to a plastic-like film; however, it will also mask surface details to some extent.

There are numerous protective finishes available, such as varnish, polyurethane, and epoxy. Lacquer is now available in two different formulations: solvent and water-based. Solvent-based products dominated the market for many years, but recent environmental concerns have prompted the development of water-based finishes.

Solvent-based finishes are generally flammable, whereas water-based products are not. Another advantage of water-based finishes is that they do not emit toxic solvents into the atmosphere unless sprayed, allowing them to meet increasingly stringent air quality standards in states such as California.

The techniques used to prepare and apply a water-based finish may differ from those used for its solvent-based counterpart. When mixing and applying a topcoat, always follow the manufacturer's instructions.

Regardless of the finish you choose, applying it requires more than slapping on a few drops and letting them dry. The wood surface must be properly prepared as follows: Filling the grain of an open-pore species, such as oak, is required before applying the finish.

A sealer coat may be necessary before applying a lacquer topcoat to an open-pore wood surface. Finally, if changing the color of the piece is part of your game plan, you will need to bleach or stain it ahead of time.

Make sure that any filler, wash coat, or stain is completely dry before preparing your tools and opening up your finish comprise. As a final step, go over the wood surfaces with a tack cloth to remove any sanding particles and dust.

The procedures for applying a topcoat vary depending on the product and application technique used.

Oils for Drying

Drying oils, which include linseed, tung, and walnut oil, are a type of natural finish that cures to form a hard film on a wood surface. Tung oil, also known as China wood oil, is a common drying oil finish. The oil is extracted from the nut of the tung tree and is available in pure, modified, and polymerized forms.

Pure tung oil is an excellent choice for finishing children's toys and eating utensils such as salad bowls because it contains no additives. Check the label if you intend to use it to ensure that the contents are 100 percent pure.

The main advantage of modified tung oils is that they contain chemical additives that allow them to dry faster. Polymerized tung oil is subjected to a special heat treatment, which causes it to dry faster and develop a glossier sheen. Drying oils are reactive finishes, which means they dry and harden when exposed to air—even if the container is sealed.

When storing drying oil, use the smallest container possible to reduce the amount of air to which the oil is exposed.

Chapter Forty Three

Varnishing Coating

Varnish is a long-lasting protective coating for wood that is more resistant to heat and alcohol damage than shellac and lacquer. It is also simple to apply, whether by brushing or using spray tools.

When brushing, try to work with a white wall or a window behind the workpiece. The reflected light will help you see if you are skipping a section or picking up dust.

Varnishes used to be made from natural resins and oils such as linseed oil. These materials have since been replaced by synthetic resins, but the old system of classifying varnish based on the oil-to-resin ratio remains in use.

As a result, varnishes are classified as short, medium, or long oil. Long oil varnish dries slowly, leaving a soft and elastic coating.

The short oil varnish is hard and glossy, and it is resistant to abrasion. In terms of gloss and resilience, medium oil varnish falls somewhere in the middle.

Brushing Application Sequence

1. Dilute the varnish and apply a thin coat to the surface with a high-quality bristle brush, working against and with the grain.
2. Allow the surface to dry for 12 to 24 hours.
3. Sand the surface with 240 or 280-grit self-lubricating sandpaper.
4. Repeat steps 1 through 3 using a stronger varnish dilution and sanding the surface with finer grit sandpaper (280 to 320-grit).
5. Apply an undiluted coat of varnish.
6. Allow the surface to dry before sanding with 400-grit sandpaper.
7. Steps 5 and 6 should be repeated two or three times.
8. Allow the finish to cure for 24 to 72 hours before rubbing it out.

Spraying Application Sequence

1. Dilute the varnish to the desired viscosity.
2. Use a low-pressure spray gun to reduce overspray and pooling.
3. Apply a thin coat of paint to the surface.
4. Allow the surface to dry before sanding with 320-grit sandpaper.
5. Steps 3 and 4 should be repeated two or three times.
6. Allow the finish to cure for 24 to 72 hours before rubbing it out.

Chapter Forty Four

How to Use Polyurethane

Polyurethane is a clear, varnish-like finish that is long-lasting, abrasion-resistant, and simple to apply.

It dries faster than varnish because it is made with synthetic resin, making it an excellent choice when finishing work is limited. Polyurethane, like varnish, can be brushed or sprayed on furniture. Polyurethanes are available in a range of lusters, from flat to glossy.

Water-based polyurethanes are safer for the environment than solvent-based polyurethanes because they do not emit toxic solvents into the atmosphere while drying.

If you intend to spray water-based polyurethane, keep your spray tools clean; oil will contaminate the water-based product.

Brushing Application Sequence
1. Using a paintbrush or a pad applicator, apply a thin and even coat, always brushing with the grain.
2. Allow the surface to dry for approximately 2 hours.
3. Using 320- to 400-grit sandpaper, sand the surface.
4. Repeat steps 1 through 3, abrading the surface with finer grit sandpaper each time.
5. Apply a final coat and wait for 18 to 24 hours before rubbing out the finish.

Spraying Application Sequence
1. Spray the work piece with varnish, allowing 30 to 60 minutes for the coat to dry.
2. Using 320 to 400-grit sandpaper, sand the surface.
3. Apply two more coats, abrading the surface after each application with progressively finer grit sandpaper.
4. Let the finish dry for at least 18 to 24 hours before rubbing it out.

CHAPTER FORTY FIVE

HOW TO APPLY SHELLAC

Shellac is a natural finish made from the secretions of the lac insect, which is found in Indochina and India. The bugs consume sap from trees and expel resin, which forms a protective shell around their bodies.

This material eventually accumulates and is deposited on tree twigs and branches, where it is harvested and processed. Shellac is available in both liquid and flakes form in the commercial market. Although liquid shellac is ready to use, flakes must first be blended with denatured alcohol.

In some ways, however, the flakes are the more convenient form of the product because you can prepare only as much of the solution as you need for a specific project.

Both types of shellac are available in a wide range of colors, from dark brown and orange to blond and white. Shellac is also classified by its "pound cut," which refers to the amount of resin present in the solvent.

1-pound cut shellac, for example, contains one pound of resin per gallon of solvent. Shellac is graded differently depending on where and when it was harvested.

Coarse shellac contains twigs and bugs, whereas super-refined shellac is almost pure liquid. While shellac provides a long-lasting finish that protects wood from humidity and abrasion, it is not resistant to water, alcohol, or heat.

Shellac, like other solvent-release finishes, forms a milky cloud on a surface known as blushing when sprayed in high humidity or with excessive moisture in the solvent. Keep the solvent in a tightly closed container.

Brushing Application Sequence

1 - Purchase or make a 1 or 2-pound-cut shellac to apply two or three wash coats to the surface. Brush the finish on quickly and evenly, using as few strokes as possible and working only with the grain. Brushstrokes should not be overlapping.

2 - Allow the surface to dry for at least 2 hours.

3 - Sand the surface with 360 or 400-grit self-lubricating sandpaper. Remove sanding particles.

4 - Apply another coat of 3-pound-cut shellac and sand.

5 - Apply three or more coats of 5-pound-cut shellac, sanding between coats.

6 - Allow 24 to 72 hours for the finish to dry before rubbing it out.

Spraying Application Sequence

1 - Prepare a spraying solution of the appropriate consistency according to the manufacturer's instructions; a 1 or 2-pound-cut shellac is typical. If using liquid shellac, you may need to dilute it.

2 - Set the spray gun for a light coat to avoid drips and runs.

3 - Apply two or three coats of wash.

4 - After about 30 minutes, sand the surface with a self-lubricating 360 or 400-grit sandpaper. Remove sanding particles.

5 - Apply three or four more coats of a more concentrated solution, sanding between applications.

6 - Allow 48 to 72 hours for the finish to dry before rubbing out.

Chapter Forty Six

How to Use Lacquer

Lacquer has been used as a protective finish for wood furniture for over 2000 years in the Far East, but it did not become popular in the West until the 17th century. The first lacquers used during China's Chou dynasty were made from natural resins; modern products are made synthetically.

Lacquer can be brushed onto a surface, but make sure to use a brush with bristles set in rubber, or the finish's solvent will cause the tool to shed. Lacquer's quick drying time also makes it ideal for spraying.A lacquer topcoat hardens to a clear, long-lasting finish. It is an excellent choice for furniture that will be subjected to water or high heat.

Unlike polyurethanes and varnishes, which form new layers with each application, lacquer dissolves the previous coats to form a single film. Finishers usually try to stick to four coats of lacquer. However, these are typically applied in addition to one or two coats of sanding sealer. The more densely a lacquer finish is built up, the more likely it will crack.

However, achieving a mirror-like lacquer finish on species such as rosewood or oak may require up to ten applications.

Finishers in ancient China were known to coat a single piece of furniture with more than 300 coats. They would carefully abrade the surface after each new application had dried to prevent cracking, and they would keep each coat as thin as possible.

Lacquer is available in a variety of sheens ranging from flat to glossy. There are also various tints to choose from, as well as a clear formulation that highlights the grain and color without changing the hue.

Brushing Application Sequence

1 - Apply the sanding sealer to the workpiece after diluting it according to the manufacturer's instructions. Allow drying before sanding with 320-grit paper.

2 - Dilute the lacquer with a retarding solvent according to the manufacturer's instructions. The retarder prevents the lacquer from drying too quickly.

3 - Apply the finish to the workpiece with a soft, long-bristled brush. Brush with the grain while working at a 45-degree angle to the surface.

Brushstrokes should not be overlapping.

4 - Allow the lacquer to dry for 2 hours before sanding with a self-lubricating 360- to 400-grit sandpaper. Remove sanding particles.

5 - Repeat steps 2–4 with a slightly more concentrated lacquer solution.

6 - Add at least two or three more coats. Brushing undiluted lacquer on the surface is not recommended; at the very least, a small amount of retarder should be added to the lacquer.

7 - Allow at least 24 hours for the finish to dry before rubbing it out.

Spraying Application Sequence

1 - Apply the sanding sealer to the workpiece after diluting it according to the manufacturer's instructions. Allow drying before sanding with 320-grit paper.

2 - Prepare a diluted lacquer solution with the manufacturer's recommended solvent and spray it onto the surface. Use a viscosity cup to ensure the lacquer has the proper consistency for spraying.

3 - Allow about an hour for the finish to dry.

4 - Sand with 320-grit self-lubricating paper.

5 - Repeat steps 2 and 3 while lightly sanding the surface. This is an optional step.

6 - Apply at least three more coats, diluting each application with a small amount of retarder and sanding the surface with 360-grit paper in between.

7 - Allow the finish to completely dry before rubbing it out.

CHAPTER FORTY SEVEN

FINISHING BY HAND

There are three basic methods for applying protective finishes by hand: wiping it on with a cloth or sponge, padding it on, or using a brush.

The technique you use should be determined by the type of finish you are using. Wiping is the best way to apply a drying oil, for example. Brushes are preferable for applying varnish, polyurethane, shellac, and lacquer.

Some finishing products, known as padding finishes, are designed to be padded onto a surface; they provide a luster similar to that of French polished or lacquered wood with far less effort.

Nonetheless, because these finishes do not easily build up into a thick coating, they require a significant amount of time and effort to apply.

As a result, they are most commonly used to repair damaged finishes. They work best as decorative details, turnings, or small pieces on newly built furniture. Apply a sealer coat of varnish, shellac, or lacquer first to reduce the amount of time required to build up a padding finish.

Wet a clean cloth or sponge with the finish and apply a thin coat to the surface. Make sure to completely cover the wood surfaces.

Allow the finish to soak into the wood for a few minutes before wiping away the excess with another clean cloth. Check the manufacturer's instructions for drying times before applying subsequent coats.

Make a finishing pad out of linen and wool, just like you would for French polishing. Pour a small amount of the finish onto the pad, then tap it against the palm of your hand to dampen it evenly.

Wipe the pad across the surface in the grain direction.
Overlap your strokes until the entire workpiece is covered and the surface has a smooth glossy sheen.

Consult the manufacturer's instructions for drying times before applying additional coats. Padding finishes are typically applied in stages.

Set the workpiece a little higher than your work surface so you can cover the wood to the bottom without slopping the finish on the table.

Prop the corners on wood blocks with small nails driven through them for a store-bought stand. Dip about one-third of the bristle length in the finish and brush along the grain, leaving behind thin, even coats if using a bristle brush.

If you apply the finish too thickly, the liquid will run, sag, or pool. Use as few brushstrokes as possible to avoid air bubbles and lap marks on the surface.

Remove any stray bristles from the finish with tweezers before it dries. Lap marks can be reduced by using a foam brush.

Chapter Forty Eight

Cleaning and Storage

A finishing project is not complete until you have cleaned and stored your brushes, stored the solvents, and disposed of any oily rags. Unlike foam brushes, which are typically discarded after a single use, bristle brushes and pad applicators can be cleaned and reused.

A high-quality brush can last for many years when properly cared for. However, good cleaning habits are important for more than just protecting your investment; they are also important for shop safety and environmental responsibility.

To keep finished goods out of the reach of children, store them in a locked metal cabinet. Throwing wet, oily rags in the trash increases the likelihood that they will catch fire.

Darken the rags and place them in a sealed rental container for temporary storage. This will protect the thorn from sparks or flames and quickly deprive any spontaneous fire of oxygen.

The safest way to dispose of oily rags is to spread them out in the open. Finishing merchandise should be kept in properly labeled, sealed containers.

Avoid using bottles or jars that normally contain food or liquids; a customer may mistake a chemical product for something drinkable. Always keep stains and finishes at room temperature; freezing a water-based product will ruin it.

Reactive finishes, such as tung oil or varnish, should be stored in airless containers because they eventually harden when exposed to air.

Instead of storing a small amount of a reactive finish in a large container. Transfer the product to a smaller container so that the liquid is exposed to less air.

Buying finishing goods in smaller quantities or storing them in collapsible plastic containers is a better solution. No finishing product should be flushed down the drain. Even water-based finishes can cause problems by clotting in drain pipes and backing up.

Improve your plumbing system

Allow small amounts of a product to sit in an uncovered container outside until the solvent evaporates. Consult your community's waste disposal service for larger volumes.

Additional Suggestions

Standing a brush on its bristles can permanently bend them and ruin the brush. Break in a new brush by immersing it up to the ferrule in a solvent compatible with the finish you'll be using.

Soak the bristles in warm water for about 10 minutes before cleaning the brush with detergent. Wrap a new or used brush in the paper after breaking it in or cleaning it.

Soak the bristles of a hardened brush overnight in a mixture of 2 parts xylene, 1 part acetone, and 1-part denatured alcohol. To remove hardened finish fragments from the bristles, use a brush comb.

Pour or brush water-based finish onto cardboard scraps to dispose of them; let them dry and discard the cardboard. Instead of throwing away an empty container of mineral spirits, recycle it. Allow the solvent to sit in a cool place for a week or two, then decant the spirits that have risen to the surface into a clean container and discard the residue.

It's pointless to clean a brush if you intend to use it the next day. Instead, soak the brush in the appropriate solvent for the finishing product. A mixture of turpentine and varnish for varnish; denatured alcohol for shellac; lacquer thinner for lacquer; and a "brush keeper" solution of 2 parts raw linseed oil and 1 part turpentine for stain.

Simply wrap the brush in plastic wrap for oil-based finishing products. When soaking a brush, immerse only the bristles, not the ferrule, and keep them suspended above the bottom of the container. Keep the brush in a commercial brush bucket or a shop-made rack by hanging it from a nail.

Chapter Forty Nine

How to Clean the Brush

1 - Cleaning the brush with solvent

Submerge the bristles of the brush in the appropriate solvent for the finishing product. Swirl the brush in the solvent, pressing the bristles against the container's sides. Working the solvent through the bristles with your hands until the brush is clean, wash the bristles in a solution of mild detergent and warm water, then pull a brush comb through them as many times as necessary.

2 - Brush spinning

Shake the brush by hand or use a brush spinner to remove the solvent. Hold the brush inside a 5-gallon can in both cases to catch the solvent as it sprays from the bristles. Insert the brush handle into the spinner and, while holding the brush in the can, pump the handle to start it spinning. Continue until no more solvent is flying off the brush.

3 - Keeping a brush

A clean brush can be kept indefinitely. Wrap the bristles in the thick, absorbent paper several times. Avoid using plastic wrap because it will prevent the bristles from drying properly and may cause them to become limp. The paper should completely cover the bristles, extending beyond the tips and over the ferrule. Hold the wrapper in place with a rubber band, making sure the elastic grips the ferrule rather than the bristles. Dry the brush by hanging it up.

Printed in the USA
CPSIA information can be obtained
at www.ICGtesting.com
LVHW051107260924
792214LV00001B/22

9 783988 319890